THE ULTIMA

CW00707998

OVERCOMING

SEXUAL AND

CHILDHOOD

ABUSE

by Liz Adamson

THE ULTIMATE GUIDE TO OVERCOMING SEXUAL AND CHILDHOOD ABUSE.

by Liz Adamson

Published by Diviniti Publishing Ltd
83, Birling Rd, Leybourne, Kent ME19 5HZ
Tel: 01732 220373
Email admin@hypnosisaudio.com
Website: www.hypnosisaudio.com

ISBN 1 901923 52 5

1st Edition

Cover image by Diane Frost

This book is dedicated to all my clients who have suffered abuse in thanks for the help and understanding they have given me that has enabled me to write this book.

CONTENTS

INTRODUCTION

I was moved to write this book due to the sheer number of clients who come to my practice and have been abused, most particularly sexually abused. You may think that this is not unusual given that I am a therapist. However, sexual abuse is rarely the issue that they have come to see me about. The subject is often only presented as an incidental or side issue and may not seem to be that important to them.

Childhood abuse is a huge problem that is not being addressed. The legacy of abuse is destroying the very foundations of our society. The amount of abuse that we are aware of is just the tip of the iceberg. Statistics suggest that up to one in three people may have been sexually abused. This is potentially one third of the world's population. Probably the majority of these people are going about their everyday lives without having told a living soul about what they have endured, such is the shame attached to this form of abuse. There may not be many outward scars that can be seen but the unhealed wounds inside will often have an adverse effect in virtually every area of life.

For many years sexual abuse has been such a taboo subject that it was not understood or addressed. Indeed, many people would not have even been aware of the possibility. Only now are people beginning to break the silence and stand up and acknowledge what has gone on. This problem is not associated with any particular race, colour or creed. It occurs in virtually every culture, religion and society across the planet. It cannot be blamed on poverty or ignorance because it is rife in all strata of society. The abusers do not fall into any specific age range, they may be anything from ten to a hundred years old. It is not only men who do the abuse, women and other children may be the perpetrators. There is nothing that singles an abuser out from anyone else. They may be pillars of society and well respected in the work place. We may be in blissful ignorance of them living next door or even within our own home!

I must stress that I do not tackle this subject based on my own personal experience of it. However, having worked with hundreds who have had to deal with it, I began to see certain patterns and similarities emerging. The negative effects of the abuse would show themselves again and again.

For many people who have been abused, it ruins their lives. This cannot be underestimated. However, I do believe that it is perfectly possible to clear these issues and to move on from the abuse without carrying any baggage or wounds. In order for this to occur, the individual needs to be willing to look at and deal with the issue and release any residue that has been created from it.

My intention in writing this book is to provide an understanding of the subject as well as the tools needed to heal the destructive elements created by the abuse. I am well aware that the vast majority of people who have suffered abuse would not dream of coming to someone like me in order to deal with the problem. It is important that everyone is given the opportunity to deal with and heal the issue without needing to air it publicly. There may be a pattern of closing ranks in order to protect the family and not betray the people involved.

In my opinion it is not enough to simply face and admit to the abuse. You can talk about it until the cows come home but it doesn't actually change anything. The problem often goes very deep and it is only by getting to the source of it that we can be be totally set free from it.

I will be dealing with the various forms of abuse separately as they create different patterns and issues within us. I will be concentrating on sexual abuse as this is by far the most common, insidious and destructive form of abuse and if it is not dealt with, the legacy of it will have far reaching consequences.

This book is in two parts. Part one looks at all the issues and patterns that are born out of abuse and part two gives the necessary tools to heal and release them.

I would ask anyone who is suffering the effects of abuse that they give themselves the gift of overcoming the issue and allowing themselves to live the wonderful and positive lives that they so richly deserve. I trust that this book provides the means by which to do this.

PART I

UNDERSTANDING THE ISSUES AROUND SEXUAL AND CHILDHOOD ABUSE

SEXUAL ABUSE

POWER AND CONTROL

It is true to say that with sexual abuse the issue is not about sex, it is about **POWER**. The abuser is coming from a position of powerlessness and is therefore looking to gain a sense of power by rendering another person powerless. However, the feeling of power gained from the abuse is short lived and very soon he will need to get another fix.

Sexual abusing is a form of addiction and like any addiction, the perpetrator will be aware that it is unhealthy and destructive but the compulsion to repeat the actions will be stronger than this awareness. This is very similar to alcoholics and drug addicts who know they are destroying themselves and their families but this does not stop them from drinking or taking drugs. Once again I will stress that with sexual abuse the addiction is to the feeling of power and not sex itself. Indeed these people may have a fairly low sex drive within their ordinary lives.

It is the need for power and feelings of powerlessness that drive an abuser to choose the most vulnerable and sensitive of targets who are not going to stand up to them or report to other adults what is happening to them. The abuser seems to have a built in radar that is able to determine this and only on very rare occasions will they get it wrong.

The need for power may also drive an abuser to take on jobs or roles in the community that give him a sense of authority and power at the same time as bringing him into contact with potential victims in a legitimate way.

Control is another area that goes hand in hand with power and has very similar patterns behind it. Abusers may be very controlling or manipulative in their everyday lives, there may even be a bully mentality. This makes people scared of them and allows them to wield their power and control with impunity.

Within the pattern of control there will be feelings of being out of control in the world or having had someone in the past who used control over them. There may seem to be only two options; to control or be controlled. Consequently, this destructive pattern passes on and on. When this cycle is at its most extreme, it can cause untold misery for families, employees and people in the wider community.

The fact is that no one has any power or control over us unless we give it to them. If we choose not to play the game, there is nothing that can be done. This is something that many of us learn as we grow up but it is not a concept that children are aware of. This is why they become the easy targets for abusers.

In healing the issues around sexual abuse, it is essential that we take our power back from those who we have given it to. This will often involve more than one person. When we take our power back, we begin to see how very weak, pathetic and powerless these people were. We might have built them up to be ogres in our minds and fed that image with our fear.

There is a vast difference between internal and external power. External power is what we try to get through money, position, status or control. Our internal power is our generator within and if we give it away, we dwindle our personal power resources. Internal power seeks to empower others while external power will disempower people. Once we have given away our internal power, we try to get it back through external power. This ultimately only reinforces our lack of power because we realise that no matter how much we achieve materially or in status, it doesn't actually give us back our inner power. When we feel internally powerful, we have no need for any external show of power.

Once again this is the addiction for power showing itself in a different guise. An addiction is always about trying to fill the emptiness inside. To an extent this void is created by giving away our inner power. When we reclaim personal power, the emptiness does not exist and consequently any need to feed it externally ceases as well.

In healing sexual abuse issues, we may need to look at how our addictions are manifesting and dealing with and understanding how power works in our individual lives.

COMMON PATTERNS WITHIN SEXUAL ABUSE

Sexual abuse is one of the biggest problems facing the world today and it is not being addressed. It is the underlying cause of many things that are blighting our society and our ability to grow and evolve in the world. This is something that is thought to have affected up to one in three people directly. However, if we take into account the indirect damage on relationships and families, the toll is incalculable.

People who have been abused will often think that they have been singled out for this punishment and that it is personal to them. It is important to get over in this book a sense of the vast sister and brotherhood that they belong to and that all these millions of other people share the same feelings and experiences. It always amazes me when I talk to people in my practice who have been abused, how similar their stories are. It is almost as if there is an unwritten code that is being played out time and again.

I will reveal here some of the common threads that run through most patterns of abuse. I will go into more detail with many of them later in the book.

1) It is more common for men to sexually abuse than women. It is certainly not unheard of for women to abuse but I would say that in about 90% of cases the perpetrator is a man.

2) Virtually all sexual abusers have been abused themselves. I must stress here that this does not mean that all those who have been abused will go on to abuse. A percentage will do so but we all have free choice.

3) Boys and girls are equally likely to be abused. Some abusers will abuse girls, some boys and many will abuse both sexes. This is regardless of the sexual orientation of the perpetrator. Remember, the issue is about power and not sex.

4) The most common ages for the abuse to occur is between six and twelve. Having said this, it is not uncommon for babies and toddlers to be abused and in some cases the abuse may go on until the person is seventeen or eighteen. It is ironic that the abuse often stops when the child reaches puberty and becomes a sexual being. This further reinforces the understanding that sex is not the central issue.

5) The abuse will usually stop when the child says NO. With age comes understanding and a realisation of the consequences to the abuser if the secret is revealed.

6) It is not unusual to try to bury memories of the abuse. In so doing it may be necessary to lock away huge chunks of childhood. When people do not remember things over the age of five, it is usually an indication that there were issues that it is safer to forget. I must stress that this is not necessarily sexual abuse. There are many other issues that may have blighted childhood.

7) There are often patterns of self-abuse that occur once the sexual abuse has ceased. This may take many different forms and I will go into further details later.

8) It is quite common for people to be abused by more than one person. This may be understandable when there is a family pattern of abuse. However this is also common when the abuse occurs in the wider community. It is as if there is some kind of sign up that indicates that this person is available for potential abusers.

9) Family patterns of abuse can pass down through many generations. It is not uncommon for a child to be abused by up to three generations of family members, for instance, grandfather, uncle and brother.

10) There is often a pattern of collusion where everyone involved goes to great lengths to present a "normal" front to the world. Often those families that appear to be happy and close to the outside world are harbouring secrets that are very different.

11) Denial can be very common in abuse patterns. If the secret is brought out into the open, many family members go into denial rather than face and deal with the issues. This can create further hurt and isolation for the one who revealed it.

12) People who have been abused will often see the need to protect themselves in later life. They may don a tough or prickly outer shell that keeps most people at bay. They may appear to be difficult or hostile. To me this is often the clearest outer indication of abuse that we see. More on this later.

13) An abuser will usually abuse many different people and on many occasions. This is why the legacy of abuse is so big. For every person who has been abused and becomes an abuser, they may pass the pain and destruction onto dozens of children who may in turn self-abuse or abuse others. It does not take a mathematician to work out how many people will be affected in future generations!

THE LEGACY OF ABUSE

I would like to address in greater detail the destructive legacy of abuse that is only getting worse as time goes by. I believe that it is only through awareness and education that we can stop the rot that is destroying the very fabric of the family, the church, the education and social systems.

Where there is sexual abuse, it is as if the baton of abuse is passed on to the victim that will either materialise most commonly as some form of self- abuse or will be turned into abusing others. Very few people emerge from this pattern unscathed. We have to learn to drop the baton and not to perpetuate the pattern still further.

One of the reasons why the pattern of abusing others occurs more often in men and self-abuse is a more common trait in women lies in the way male and female energies work. I am not talking about men and women here but masculine and feminine energy. We all, regardless of our gender work with both these energies and the ratio of them within us will determine what part of the male/female spectrum we fit into. Ideally, we are meant to be a balance of the two, working with the positive aspects of both.

Male energy tends to be more outward, men are the providers, the hunter gatherers and their focus is more on the external world. Female energy is more inward, it is based on emotions rather than thoughts, it is intuitive, creative and nurturing. If we put this understanding into the abuse issue, we can see that an excess of male energy will project the pattern outwardly onto others where the female energy will take it inwardly and put it onto the self. We can see this occurring with the energy of anger. Male energy sends it out as aggression, while female energy is more likely to turn it inward against the self, this is depression. Once again I will stress that I am not referring to men and women here but to male and female energies. Many women work with male energy as men do with female energy.

Patterns are usually set on an unconscious level and they are equally unconscious when they are passed on. It is as if we are robots that have been given a certain program that plays out with various feelings, thoughts and actions. Sometimes we may consciously not want to feel, think or act in this way but the compulsion to do so may seem stronger than our will to stop. We are not robots and we do have the gift of free choice and will. However, it may be necessary to remove and delete this powerful program before we are able to live the way in which we choose.

This pattern does not just apply in the arena of sexual abuse; it is affecting us in many areas of life. When a pattern is set, we feel compelled to follow it and do as we have done before, no matter how much we may want to do it differently. If we do not remove the program and the pattern, we will create a huge internal battle that will play out each time we are faced with the pattern. Unless we have enormous will power, the pattern will usually win out. In part two of this book there is a process to remove the program and pattern.

In my experience we only manage to consistently go against a pattern for a few weeks before we revert back to our old ways. I see this most commonly in relationships where the pattern is threatening to split them up. Promises to change the pattern of behaviour will only succeed for a limited period and a great deal of energy is used in the process. If we want to change a program, we have to do it within.

It takes a conscious decision for each person who is carrying the baton and legacy of abuse to let it go and heal themselves at the same time as choosing not to pass it on to a living soul knowing the misery that it creates.

For those people who use the abuse against themselves there is often an understanding that it doesn't matter if they hurt themselves as long as no one else is getting hurt. This is often an indication of how low their sense of self-worth is. There are always going to be people who love us who are greatly affected by our self-destructive behaviour. We have only to look at the suffering caused in families of drug addicts or alcoholics. Nobody is unscathed by this. The fact is that if we believe ourselves to be unworthy of love, we will not let the love of our nearest and dearest in and they will feel hurt and rejected as a result.

THE SPECTRUM OF SEXUAL ABUSE

Sexual abuse covers a vast spectrum of experience. It may seem as if we cannot compare a single incident of molestation by a stranger to years of sexual abuse from a close family member. However, it would be a mistake to dismiss what may seem like a minor incident and think that it has not affected us in any way.

Within the actual act of sexual abuse there are also a variety of actions from inappropriate touching to full intercourse or rape that come under the same umbrella. Strangely, sometimes it is not the severity of the abuse that dictates the damage created by it. Each individual will have their own responses and cocktail of issues that are born out of their experience.

I will address as much as possible the different aspects of sexual abuse. There may be a voyeuristic side to it or it may be more about what the perpetrator gets the child to do to him rather than the other way round.

I have broken down the areas of sexual abuse into three separate categories because the effects will be different within each one.

1) Abuse within the family.

2) Abuse in the wider community. This occurs when the person is known to the child. It may be a neighbour, teacher, priest, friend of the family or parent of a friend.

3) Abuse by a stranger. This includes rape.

SEXUAL ABUSE WITHIN THE FAMILY

This is by far the most damaging area of sexual abuse there is. It brings into play far more issues than just the abuse itself. If the abuser is a father, brother or close relative there is the whole taboo subject of incest to be taken into account. The closer the familial relationship, the greater the damage created from it. Many times the abuser is a step father, step grandfather or uncle by marriage. This puts the abuse in the family but it is not a blood relative that has committed it.

I think it is hardest for people to deal with abuse when it is a father who is inflicting it upon them. Here the sacred trust of the parent to love and nurture the child is broken in a big way. Where a father is involved, there will be hugely conflicting emotions. This is a person that the child loves and wants love from who is doing this. Some children may find that the only form of affection that they receive from that parent may occur within the abuse and this may represent the attention that they are craving. The father may be very strict or controlling in other areas of life and appear more loving or approachable during the abuse.

A child being abused by a father may often attract a great deal of jealousy from other members of the family. It is common for a mother to resent any signs of intimacy between the father and child and other siblings may see it as an indication of favouritism. These dynamics add further complications to the situation and may isolate the child even more in the family.

When a father abuses his child it is an act of betrayal. The legacy is that it is unable to totally trust anyone ever again and the one place that should represent a haven of safety and security becomes the most dangerous place for it. Children often think that their mothers are aware of the situation and are choosing to condone it.

There will be enormous amounts of anger for an abusive father and most of this anger will not be able to be expressed. We are taught to honour our fathers and mothers but how are we allowed to react when they do not honour us?

Many people experience sexual abuse at the hands of more than one family member. The pattern of abuse is so strong that brothers who have also been abused by the same relative as the younger child will often be looking to get back their sense of power and control by abusing it. I have seen many cases where two or three brothers or even sisters will abuse the younger sibling. This compounds the sense of being a victim and reinforces any belief that the abuse was deserved.

Difficult as it may be to believe, many abused children bury the memory of their abuse. This can occur even when multiple abusers are involved. This is a very powerful, unconscious survival technique that the body employs in order to cope. We have to continue to live within the family and probably see the abuser on a regular basis. This would be nigh on impossible if all the feelings and damage from the abuse were on the surface. Many children develop a technique where they totally disconnect while the abuse is taking place so many of the details are out of their reach. However, anything that is toxic to our systems has a way of finding its way to the surface. For many people the memories begin to emerge in their late teens or twenties. Different things will prove to be the trigger for this. It may be watching a drama or reading a book and seeing the experience recreating itself. It might be a smell or a phrase that sets it off. A very common trigger for memories is our own children. When we see them at the same age as we were when the abuse took place, it may awaken the incidents in our minds. A client of mine was measuring the height of her daughters against a door frame and she saw herself at a similar height and memories of the abuse came flooding back.

Once the memories begin to return, it is like putting a jigsaw puzzle together. One thing leads to another and gradually the whole sorry picture emerges. It is very easy to go a bit off the rails at this point, it may feel as if the abuse is happening all over again. Unlike people who have a retained memory, it explodes into their consciousness along with all the fierce emotions attached to it.

When the images and flash backs begin to emerge, it is quite common to be unable to put a face to the abuser, there may be an unwillingness to deal with knowing that someone close has done this. Some people may even put the wrong face to the image rather than admit who it was. There has been a great deal of adverse publicity about something called "false memory syndrome." The belief is that the imagination creates these memories of abuse and poor innocent members of the family get accused of something they have not done. I think it is really quite rare for people to completely make up these memories. There may be many instances where perhaps the wrong person is blamed because of circumstances. Most abusers will deny their crime until presented with irrefutable proof. This proof is rarely in existence and so it is always going to be the word of the child against the adult and this carries little weight legally. It is often only when two or more people come forward with a similar tale that anything is taken seriously. One of the hardest things is to get an abuser to admit what he has done and sometimes this is all that the victim is looking for.

There are huge patterns of denial associated with all areas of abuse. Many people who have been abused would never allow this information out. The abuser will deny what he has done and many other members of the family who have not been directly involved will deny that it ever happened. A huge amount of anger and pain is caused when a mother or close member of the family continues to consort with the abuser even when the fact has come out into the open. The message to the victim is that he or she doesn't matter and there is no loyalty being given to the child. The fact is that denial is a very powerful thing. It can avoid seeing things that are obvious to anyone else. When abuse is revealed in the family, the whole family may go into denial over it. The person abused will often be blamed for the family disintegration and be ostracised from the family.

I think that one of the most difficult decisions to make is whether to bring the abuse out into the open or indeed whether to report it to the police or authorities. There is no rule of thumb here as each case is different. The priority has got to be that the person abused works through the issues and releases themselves from the destructive bondage of the abuse. The next point to consider is whether other people are in danger of being abused by this person. If they are working with children, fostering or brought into contact with children, it may be necessary to inform the correct authorities who may be able to protect the interests of those children. Consider how you would feel if innocent children suffered the same fate as you because you did not prevent it. When the children at risk are the offspring of the abuser himself, this may be a different kettle of fish. It would not be a good idea to go in with hobnail boots and make accusations that may not be true. I think the best approach here may be to empower the children involved. To let them know that they have the power to say no to anything they do not want to happen and that they can come to you if they are concerned about anything. This can be done without alarming them or going into too much detail. There have been many instances where children have been put into care to remove them from sexual abuse but this makes them feel like they are being punished and they are often further abused in care either by workers or other inmates who have been abused. I believe that the solution to this problem is not to destroy families further but to use education, awareness and empowerment. Breaking the family apart does not help everyone involved to deal with their issues and put a stop to the pattern of abuse.

When confronting the subject in the family, it is a good idea to start with the siblings. This applies to both boys and girls. Just be aware that they may or may not have been abused themselves and they may or may not be ready to admit it. Do not push too hard as this may be met with defence or aggression. Consult together whether it would be productive to bring the information to other members of the family. Use intuition to decide whether this would be the right action. There may be a big can of worms that is being opened that cannot be contained. Sometimes it is easier to put what we want to say in writing and the feelings and reactions to the situation can be given without blaming other people.

Another quandary is whether to face and confront the abusers themselves. It takes a very brave person to do this. This decision is up to each individual but it may not always achieve what is desired. We often need the person or people to admit what they have done and show some remorse for it. We may be disappointed if this is what we expect. The abuser may deny it totally, accuse us of being mad, paranoid or delusional and end up making us wonder if we made the whole thing up. Again, if it feels important to present the abuser with what they have done, it may be better to do this by letter rather than in person. Have no expectations as to what will happen as a result of this but know your intention in doing so. If you want to confront them let it be part of the healing process, perhaps to provide closure so that you can move on. If you want simply to punish the person for what they have done this might backfire on you!

Abuse within the family often creates feelings of isolation and loneliness. Most victims think that they are the only people in the world that this is happening to and it is occurring because of something that is intrinsically wrong with them. One client was totally unaware that her stepfather was also abusing all her brothers and sister and was quite happy to send her own children to stay with him, never thinking that he was also abusing them. Her self-esteem was so low that she felt she must deserve this punishment but her siblings and children didn't, so it wouldn't happen to them. When we are healing the abuse, it may be helpful to get together with other people who have gone through the same thing. Sometimes when we can objectively see how undeserving they were of the abuse, we can begin to transfer this understanding to ourselves. So many people go through the whole of their lives convinced that they must have warranted the abuse or it would not have happened.

When we heal ourselves of sexual abuse to an extent we are doing it for the whole family. The main priority is to stop the whole cycle of abuse from being passed on to future generations. The buck must stop here. This includes the pattern of self-abuse as well as abusing others.

We have all been given the gift of free will and choice and this is where we have to exercise it. The greatest revenge we can take is to not let them win by destroying us. They want to bring us down to their level so that they can feel better about themselves. If we use what has happened and turn it around and make a success of our lives, we show them how weak and pathetic they truly are. Success is not measured by money or the material, it is how we feel inside. When we are at peace with ourselves, we know that we are free from any destructive aspects of abuse.

SEXUAL ABUSE IN THE WIDER COMMUNITY

In this category we are looking at abuse that takes place by people who are known to the child but are not within the family. We are only just beginning to be aware of the full extent of this problem as scandals within various institutions are coming to light. Indeed, I think we are only seeing the beginning of what is in fact a far bigger problem than anyone can imagine.

There are certain factors that allow this area of abuse to remain hidden or off limits. The people involved are often in positions of power or have big organisations behind them. The shame and guilt created by the abuse will usually be enough to stop the person from speaking out even years later.

We see the issue of power showing itself very strongly here. Children are often made to feel totally defenceless in these situations and it is very rare for them to break the code of silence because they are so intimidated by the person.

We are taught as children to be polite and have respect for our elders and betters. At no time are we ever informed that these people could abuse us or that we have the right to say no or get it stopped by reporting it to authorities. This is something that every child needs to be told in order to have the tools to face life in the outside world.

Parents are often obsessed with "stranger danger" and warning children never to talk to strangers, get in their cars or allow them to touch them or give them sweets. This is often reinforced by stories in the media that create fear and panic in parents. These incidents are actually very rare in comparison to abuse by people who are known to the child. Parents do not warn of the danger from neighbours, teachers, friends of the family or even priests and happily send the child off to face this abuse. This is another area where education and awareness needs to take place in order to prevent this problem from being allowed to continue.

Most abusers in the wider community will usually be very pleasant and normal human beings. There are no external signs that they are potential abusers. They may well make themselves indispensable to people doing good works or being involved in civic activities. Often when the abuse comes to light many people refuse to believe it as they have been nothing but charming to them. This aspect of their personality is often necessary in order to evade detection. Children think they will not be believed because this person is so well thought of in the community.

The abuser will often have to prepare the ground before the abuse can take place. This is known as "grooming." The person may befriend the potential victim. He might provide presents or treats that endear him to the child. He will be everything that he perceives it is wanting or needing. Once he has gained the child's trust he will begin to isolate and alienate it from friends and family. The is done very subtly but effectively. The abuse may only occur once all these things are in place. By this time the child will have invested a great deal of themselves in the abuser and this may ensure its silence. This process may take place on the Internet these days.

If parents can be aware of the whole "grooming" process, this could be one way of safeguarding against abuse before it takes hold. If an adult or older child is befriending a child no matter how innocent it may seem, the alarm bells should begin to ring. We need to ask ourselves why that person is not looking for friends within its own peer group.

There are some areas where abuse seems to be prevalent and I will address each of them individually. Probably the area of abuse that has most come to our attention in recent years is in the Catholic church. I myself went to a Catholic boys school and it was widely known among the pupils that certain priests were sexually abusing boys. This information was never taken to or acted upon by higher authorities and certainly no one made any attempt to get this stopped. The information is only coming out now, ten, twenty, thirty or even forty years after the event. I don't think we can begin to conceive how big this problem is. For every child that comes forward, there will be hundreds that are stuck in the pain and shame and do not want to bring it out into the public arena.

Some people believe that sexual abuse is so prevalent in the Catholic church because of enforced celibacy in the priesthood. Personally I do not think this to be the case. The issue is about power and not sex. Just as the abuse legacy in the family passes down the generations, so it does within the family of the church. I would say that many priests that abuse will most certainly have been abused and in all likelihood by a priest as a child. Such is the pattern that it will tend to recreate itself in similar ways. The program will be unconsciously activated and will become part and parcel of their role. If we think that a priest working within a school may abuse hundreds of boys over their total career. Each one of these victims will carry this emotional wound for the rest of their lives. There are many instances of these people going on to commit suicide.

I think the betrayal is so great when the abuse occurs

29

within the church because these men are perceived as being good, holy people; God's representatives here on earth. Parents entrust their children to them in the belief that they are getting the best education and care. This is also why children do not report it because the priests are held in such high esteem within the community. It is interesting to note that the abuse is often performed by priests that have reached high positions within the hierarchy. If it is a head priest who is doing the abusing then who do they get reported to? The church has received a great deal of criticism for brushing the problem under the carpet and allowing known paedophiles to continue to work with children. This gives the message that the abuser is more important than innocent children. It is the abuser that is being protected and safeguarded. Denial will probably be coming into play here. Just as in the family, it is easier to pretend that it hasn't happened than to deal with the ramifications. The church is aware of the threat that abuse poses to its very existence and the power that it has in the world.

I am not suggesting for one moment that the Catholic church is the only one displaying this pattern. Indeed, I have had clients who have been abused by representatives of the Jewish and Hindu religions and I am sure it is rife within many religious institutions.

Schools can also be places that are far from safe for children. I have know a few cases where the head master has been the abuser. I think this was exacerbated when corporal punishment was legal in schools and was up to the discretion of the head teacher. This form of punishment often stepped over a line into sexual abuse and certain masters would wield it for sexual purposes rather than as a form of discipline. This may not be occurring in schools in this day and age but there are many people out there who still bear the physical and emotional scars. It is not just teachers that children are in danger from with sexual abuse in schools. Janitors, caretakers and garden staff may also be responsible. Paedophiles will be drawn to jobs where children are to be found.

Perhaps the biggest threat to children in schools is not from teachers or adults but from older children. This is particularly rife within boarding schools. Once again this is a pattern that passes on and perpetuates. Boys who have been abused by older boys may then try and regain power and control by abusing younger, vulnerable boys. Often very little is done to address or stop this problem. Some people even brush is off with a "boys will be boys" attitude, little realising how destructive it is.

There is a huge amount of sexual abuse within the medical profession and it is not limited just to children, many adults are being sexually abused by doctors everyday. I have had countless clients who have been abused by doctors. This is a very difficult area because in certain circumstances it is permissible for doctors to touch or invade intimate areas of the body but it is hard to know exactly when that line has been stepped over. There is a huge amount of trust and power given to doctors. In the recent past they were thought of as demigods. Every parent wanted their sons to be one and their daughters to marry one. It is always dangerous to give our power away and when this is done en masse, it can make people lose touch with reality and believe that they are above the normal rules of society. Within this pattern there is an unwillingness to make a fuss or report the doctor involved. We are often vulnerable when we are unwell and there is a fear that we will not be believed or that it will be turned around and we

31

will be blamed for it or made to feel that we are making it up or are paranoid. Some patients that make a complaint about a doctor find that they have a problem getting another doctor to take them on as they are viewed as troublemakers.

Another area where there are huge amounts of abuse is with friends of the family or in the child's friends families. Parents will unsuspectingly allow their children to go into these peoples' homes thinking they will be safe and treated just as other peoples' children would be treated in their home. For most people it would be inconceivable to think that their friends would be capable of doing this and so the safeguards are just not in place.

There are instances of bringing people into the home who are not safe for the children. Some of these people are there to take care of the little ones. They may be baby sitters or child minders or even people helping within the house. Lodgers are also an area of potential abuse.

Sadly, there are numerous cases of abuse occurring in the very system that is set up to protect and care for abused, neglected and abandoned children. Childrens' homes and foster care being the most notable of these. The irony is that many of these children are removed from their own families because of abuse, only to have it reinforced by the very people who are meant to help them.

There are many instances of abuse for children in out of school activities like scouting, sports and hobby clubs. Once again the potential abusers will gravitate to these activities.

The main reason why so much abuse in the wider community is able to continue is that the children involved will rarely report it, even to friends or members of the family. Consequently, these people are not on any paedophile register and are able to take jobs or do voluntary work with children with impunity. This is often due to the threats that take place during the abuse. The abuser may tell the child that no one will believe them if they tell or that the child will be blamed and punished for his or her part in the action. Not only this but there is often a big institution or official body that may stand behind that person and seem as if it will protect them against any allegations. Sadly, this has often proved to be the case.

The solution to the problem of abuse in the wider community is to educate children to know what is appropriate and what is not and that they can say no to what does not feel right. Children also need to know that they are as important as any adult and they have rights that need to be protected. Not for one moment do I think we can protect children by removing them from anyone or anything that may be harmful to them. This would create almost as much damage to the child as the abuse would. This is why the answer lies in the hands of children and to do this we have to lift the taboos and silence surrounding this issue.

I think there is a fear that children may lie and make up stories in order to get people into trouble. The fact is that children may lie about how many sweets they have had or whether they cleaned their teeth but they rarely lie about sexual abuse. This is particularly true for children under the age of ten because their sexual awareness would not be such that they could make up the details of what has happened. Any child making a false allegation would probably have been abused by someone else.

Parents also need to be educated and learn not to be fooled by outward appearances. They have given too much power and trust away to people who hold positions of authority and status within the community. Parents can also learn to spot the signs in their children that all is not well. This may be withdrawal, aggression, an unwillingness to go to school or to do the activities that put them in contact with the abuser. So often parents override these objections and force the child to continue going. This often makes the child feel as if the parent is in collusion with the abuser.

The patterns of protection and sacrifice may also come into play here. Children are often aware of how devastated and guilty their parents would be if they knew what was going on and so they withhold the information until even years later when they themselves become adults.

SEXUAL ABUSE BY STRANGERS

Sexual abuse by strangers is rare in comparison to the other two categories and yet it will often get a great deal more media attention. Part of the reason for its rarity particularly in young children is that parents have an awareness and fear of the danger to their offspring and put in the necessary safeguards. Children do not walk to school on their own anymore. They are not allowed to play in the street unsupervised. They are taught what to do or say if a stranger approaches them. As a result of this, it is often much older children who are given more freedom that are at more risk from stranger abuse. We can learn from this that if we put in the safeguards and gave children the right tools, the other forms of abuse could be reduced drastically.

Whenever a child is abducted it makes headline news. Unfortunately, the outcome of these cases is usually tragic and it shocks the world. For a while afterwards children are kept indoors or accompanied everywhere. Even in these cases many of the abductors were known to the children. It seems strange that there is so much prevention in place where there is a relatively small risk of abuse and yet hardly any at all in the family and wider community where there is an enormous risk of abuse. I think there is often denial at work here. We like to think of perverts or paedophiles as being monsters who live in someone else's neighbourhood, we cannot equate them with members of our own family, friends or respected people in the community.

Most abuse from strangers is opportunist. The child simply happened to be in the wrong place at the wrong time. It may be the man who flashes or touches a child in the park or public toilets. Much of this form of abuse can be prevented by making sure that the abuser is not given the opportunity because the child is never alone in public. Most paedophiles would not attempt to abuse a child who is accompanied. Abuse by strangers will often get reported to the police even if it is a harmless flasher. There is not such a great sense of shame associated with stranger abuse as the other forms. The child is never perceived as asking for it or deserving of it.

The most serious form of abuse by strangers is rape. This is far more likely to happen to a teenager than a young child. However, the legacy of rape by a stranger is huge. Many people get locked into the trauma of it and find it difficult to move on from it. There may be violence and threats involved that make it physical and emotional abuse as well. Rape ruins lives and it is essential to work through all the emotional and mental aspects of it in order to be free.

When we have been raped, we feel personally violated. Rape by a stranger is never personal to us, the rapist does not know or care who or what we are. Once again, we are simply in the wrong place at the wrong time. Understanding that it is not personal and that we were not individually targeted for this abuse is essential in healing it. The issue is with the rapist and not ourselves. We may wonder how we attracted it or how we should have safeguarded against it. Sadly, there is a warped belief in some men that if a woman is out on the streets on her own at night that she is somehow asking for it. Knowing this, it is essential that the opportunity is not provided for these sick people.

Rape as in other forms of abuse is about power and not sex. Rapists are often loners and very pathetic and inadequate individuals. They will certainly have come from a very dysfunctional background with either absent or controlling parents. They may not be in any form of relationship and will often be perceived as being weird or strange by their peer group.

Many women do not report rape to the police. This is often due to the system which subjects them to medical examinations and questioning that may feel like being raped all over again. If the rapist is caught, the ensuing court case is another ordeal. They will have to see the rapist again and may be accused of encouraging or causing the attack as many defence barristers imply. Consequently, the actual instances of rape are far higher than any statistics indicate.

Many rape victims adopt the prickly tough shell to disguise and protect their fear and vulnerability and they may find it hard to let a man get close to them. Rape can often be a very brutal act and its legacy is different from abuse that happens many times or over many years. There is often shock and trauma that gets locked into the body and it is essential that this is released in order to work through the issues brought up. There has been much talk in recent years of "post traumatic stress disorder" and this would certainly be an instance where this occurs. There may be feelings of depression or rage and an inability to function in the way the victim had before.

I must stress here that a post traumatic stress reaction may occur years after the rape has taken place and consequently it is easy not to make the connection. The trauma may be triggered by something else that creates feelings of powerlessness. It may be redundancy or divorce or even childbirth.

Rape can devastate lives if it is allowed to take root and fester. This is what the rapist intended; to drag other people down to his level of powerlessness, pain and dysfunction. If we let this happen then he has won. There is nothing that happens to us that we cannot use, turn around and make the best of. We can choose not to see ourselves as victims, we can decide not to have fear and we can use our experiences to help others or raise the awareness to prevent it from happening to others.

Molestation while serious will not have the same destructive impact as rape. It may involve being touched or forced to watch or touch the perpetrator. They often do not dare go any further than this and are rarely potential rapists. Places to be aware that these people lurk are parks, playgrounds, near schools, public toilets, buses and other forms of public transport. Virtually all of these can be safeguarded against. Many of these types of abusers have gone underground and use the Internet or videos to get their kicks or fulfil the addiction through images rather than with the children themselves. This does open up a whole new can of worms where children are being used, abused and exploited to provide these images. This will usually come under the category of abuse by a person known to the child.

EMOTIONS CREATED BY SEXUAL ABUSE

GUILT

WHEN SOMEONE TAKES OUR INNOCENCE FROM US, WE PERCEIVE OURSELVES TO BE GUILTY.

Guilt is one of the most destructive emotions that there is. It is almost always internalised and there are no outward manifestations of it that are clear to the world. The reason why guilt is so devastating is that where there is a sense of guilt, there will also be a perception that we deserve to be punished. We will either give others the power to punish us or we will do it ourselves. Either way the effects will be negative.

The innocence of a child is one of the most endearing qualities there is. It is what I call positive vulnerability. When sexual abuse occurs, it will seem as if that innocence has been taken away and cannot be replaced. This is an illusion, since the innocence comes from within but part of the pattern and program of abuse is to perceive its loss on an unconscious level. If we are no longer innocent then we must be guilty.

There are many reasons why we take on guilt as a part of sexual abuse. Some of these are given by the abuser and others we take on ourselves.. There is often a sense that we must have already done something wrong and that the abuse is the punishment for it. It does not matter that we don't know what our transgressions were. We might take this even further and believe that there is something wrong with us that we are being subjected to this punishment. A major part of the healing of sexual abuse is the realisation that the abuse is not personal to us, it is never to do with us but all about the perpetrator.

The abuser will often use guilt as the weapon of control to keep the child from telling on them. He will tell the child that this is all its fault and if anyone found out it would be blamed and punished. This would often be repeated every time an incident took place, reinforcing the sense of guilt and responsibility. This threat alone is usually enough to ensure the silence of the child. Guilt and fear of discovery allows the abuser to continue.

There is another source of guilt that is perhaps harder for the child to come to terms with. An abuser will often target a child who is needy of love, affection, praise, material things and attention. Part of the abuse may involve giving the child some of these things. So there may be aspects of the encounter that are enjoyable. It may seem as if by accepting the parts that the child needs and wants, they are also agreeing to the bits they don't. They will almost feel as if they are encouraging the person and the action. There will often be enormous guilt associated with this.

Children are also very sensual. There will be parts of the abuse that may create pleasurable feelings for them. This is perfectly natural and normal but it may make the child feel as if it were wanting or asking for the abuse to take place.

A CHILD IS NEVER GUILTY OR TO BLAME FOR CREATING SEXUAL ABUSE. There are no possible circumstances where a child is responsible for the abuse. It is always down to the adult to respect the natural sexual boundaries that each one of us has.

Guilt is always a decision or choice that we make. Consequently, if we choose to feel guilty, we can also choose not to. Ironically, the abuser will rarely feel guilty for what he has done to the child. Paedophiles will often convince themselves that the children want and enjoy it, therefore they are doing them a favour. At this point they will have totally lost touch with reality and their own feelings.

Part of the healing process involves seeing that the child's innocence is still there and that there is nothing to be guilty for. We can often do this by stepping back from the situation or looking at a child of a similar age and asking "could this child ever be guilty of creating the abuse?" When we see it from the outside and not from within, we know that the answer will always be NO!

No one can ever be free from the destructive legacy of abuse until they let the guilt and associated punishment go. This may not happen overnight but it is a choice that can be made on a daily basis. I will show ways to deal with guilt in part 2.

MANIFESTATIONS OF GUILT

1) Being a people pleaser. Feeling not good enough inside and compensating for this by being everything to everybody on the outside.

2) Being a doormat. An inability to say no or create firm boundaries for those around.

3) Believing that we don't deserve good things or to be treated well.

4) A strong saboteur.

5) Destructive self-deprecating mind talk.

6) Feeling uncomfortable when someone does or gives us something.

7) Allowing life to punish us and when it doesn't we punish ourselves.

8) Choosing options that will have a negative effect on us.

9) Having certain physical conditions that involve chronic pain can have guilt at their core.

10) Feeling bad or responsible for things that have nothing to do with us.

SHAME

Shame is another emotion that is strongly associated with sexual abuse. It is another feeling that is completely internalised. We can feel as if we are burning with shame. We often experience this feeling in the solar plexus and may feel the need to cover it up.

The shame from sexual abuse may show itself in different areas. There may be a sense of shame associated with the body. This may mean that under no circumstances do we feel comfortable revealing the body even to our spouses. There may be also feelings of shame and betrayal at the body for having sensual feelings.

Within the act of sexual abuse, a child may have been exposed to or made to participate in degrading or humiliating acts that a sexually aware adult would not choose to experience. There will be an enormous amount of shame attached to these incidents.

If I put a visual picture to shame, it always seems to present itself as thick, hot, black tar. It is very corrosive to the physical body and may well attack the lower or reproductive organs. Shame needs to find release.

ANGER

Anger is understandably going to be an emotion that is strongly associated with any form of abuse. We feel anger when someone either does something we do not want or someone doesn't do something we want.

It would be very natural to feel anger towards the abuser. However, rarely is this anger expressed in a safe way or about the person who has created it. Sometimes the places and people the anger is redirected onto will create as much damage as the abuse itself. We are often afraid of the person who is abusing us and we would not want to incite them further by showing our anger to them. We will then deflect the anger onto safer targets. I will look at these in more detail.

Within abuse the bulk of our anger will often be directed onto ourselves. We have already seen that there is a strong presence of guilt and shame and what better punishment is there than our own anger. When we turn our anger against ourselves, it will feed the self-destructive behaviour and it will usually result in bouts of depression. It is very common for people who have been abused to suffer from depression. The depression will only lift when the anger is accessed and safely released without causing any further pain to anyone. When we turn our anger onto ourselves, we are only perpetuating the cycle of abuse and we become the loser.

I was working with a lady who had been sexually abused by her step-father over a number of years. She was adamant that she felt no anger towards this man. All of her anger was directed onto herself. One day I asked her how she felt if she watched a drama where a child had been abused or saw a story on the news. She said that she would feel so angry that she could kill the man who had done that to the child. She allowed herself to feel that anger on behalf of a fictional child and yet she felt that she must have somehow deserved it. It is easy to deflect our anger onto the wrong people.

Sometimes our anger at abuse gets projected onto all and sundry. Some children might take their aggression out at school, becoming bullies and passing on the power and control pattern. Anyone who seems weak or vulnerable can become a target for their anger. It is common for abused children to become wild and out of control. They will flout any form of authority, they may well drop out of school or get in with a bad crowd. All of this behaviour will be led by anger that is being directed everywhere but at the person it is about.

Later in life it is not unusual for women to take out their anger on men in general. It is as if any man should be punished for the actions of the ones who have abused her. This is unfair and can prove disastrous in relationships. What often happens is that feelings and patterns around the abuse remain dormant a great deal of the time. Then something is said or done that in some way mirrors some aspect of the abuse and anger explodes out in a dangerous and uncontrolled way. All of this anger is heaped onto the poor hapless man who had nothing to do with its creation. Any relationship will only stand so much before it breaks apart. It is a good idea to be aware of any abuse in the past of anyone we get into a relationship with. This will help to understand when these outbursts occur and learn not to take them personally.

I have observed that there is often more anger felt towards the person who failed to protect the child from the abuse than the abuser. This is usually the mother. It will seem as if she has let them down in the most basic of maternal roles, protection. It may also appear as if the mother is in collusion with the abuser, that she must be aware of what is going on but chooses to turn a blind eye and allow it to carry on. The mother might even seem to be creating situations that allow the abuser to do his thing. Once again, it is easier to be angry with a parent than it is with the abuser himself. Many families fall apart as a result of abuse and holding onto the anger at the lack of safety will often be a major factor in this. It is interesting to note that after food and warmth the most important thing a child needs is a sense of safety and security. This features above love. When the abuse occurs within the home or even in the child's bed or bedroom, this lack of safety causes untold damage to the child's psyche.

Much of our destructive behaviour in life is designed so that we do not need to feel our anger. Much of the time we try to create a buffer between ourselves and it. The most common things we use are food, cigarettes, alcohol, drugs, (prescription or otherwise) and work. These are always signs to me that a person is running away from their emotions; anger and pain being the most predominant of these. The fact is that we need to acknowledge and feel our emotions before we can let them go. Once they are released, we do not have to feel them any longer. When we try to mask the emotions, we commit ourselves to carrying them around with us and trying to avoid people and situations that may trigger them.

There are a vast number of people who live their lives in a permanent low grade depression. This state has probably been around for so long that it feels as if it is normal. These people are living at a basic survival level. Concepts like joy, happiness and laughter may be so far removed from their reality that they have no experience of them. Everyone around them will put this down to their personality or temperament. Once again, unexpressed anger will be at the source of this problem. These people are often the least angry or aggressive people you could meet. The anger is buried very deep and the effort taken to keep it there often contributes to the constant tiredness and apathy that is evident. If that anger is released, the real person behind the depression can begin to emerge. This is a pattern that occurs quite frequently in abuse cases.

Hatred is a very extreme form of anger and it is a word I often hear in relation to a person's abuser. Hatred is a very toxic emotion and if allowed to fester, will prove very destructive to the body. It is essential that feelings of hatred and anger toward the abuser are expressed and released. I am not proposing that this be done directly to the person since this is rarely productive. In part two the means by which anger can be expressed will be shown. There can only be total freedom from the abuse when the anger is dealt with and aimed at the person who created it.

MANIFESTATIONS OF ANGER

1) Depression.
2) Tiredness and apathy.
3) Anger or rage exploding over small things. e.g. road rage.
4) Spending most spare time watching television or on the computer.

5) Eating junk or sweet food.

6) Sexual disinterest.

7) Not wanting to connect with people or even look them in the eye.

8) Not wanting to exercise or do healthy things.

9) Using cigarettes, alcohol or drugs.

10) Procrastination.

11) Avoiding people or situations that might arouse the anger.

12) Can't be bothered to make an effort for anything.

13) Not being able to concentrate.

HURT AND PAIN

Hurt and pain are very closely linked with anger. Many women cry when they are angry and many men are angry when they are hurt. Abuse will create a great deal of pain on many levels.

When a child is subjected to any form of abuse, it changes who they are forever. In an idealised picture of childhood, we see kids as playing and laughing and leading a carefree existence where they are loved, nurtured and protected. Although this is an illusion, an abused child is denied the chance of living up to the ideal. At the point where the abuse first takes place, this kind of childhood is lost to the child. There is often a sense of loss and bereavement for the innocence and naivety that the child had. It is thrust into a complicated adult world where it has to quickly learn the rules in order to survive. These rules are usually provided by the abuser and consequently very warped.

Loneliness and isolation will often result from abuse and there is a great deal of pain associated with this. For many people these feelings do not subside even when they are married with a family and friends around them. The child inside remains removed and disconnected from the closeness of the family. Abuse can make one feel like an outsider who can never be part of the normal group.

There is often the greatest amount of hurt when the abuse has been perpetrated by someone who is close to us like a parent, sibling, grandparent or uncle. There is a sense of betrayal that comes into play and a great deal of confusion about love and how it manifests. Children are very generous with their love and it is especially painful when that is betrayed.

Once hurt and pain are created, we will often go to great lengths to bury it, shut it away or protect it. We do this in our emotional centre, the solar plexus. However, this is also where our vulnerability lies. I call this locking the wolf into the sheep's pen. Instead of processing and releasing the pain, we put it where it can do the most harm to us and we are terrified of anyone getting too close and letting it out.

Most of the destructive elements of hurt and pain are created by our efforts to avoid feeling it or protecting ourselves from people getting too near it. If we are willing to feel the pain for a few moments and let it process on through, not only do we not have to carry it around with us but we can be open and available to all the lovely people and experiences that life has to offer. We can learn so much from babies in how to deal with emotions. They feel them, express them and without residue are on to the next feeling. The expression is the processing and letting go.

However, there are two sorts of tears and expression of pain. The victim or "poor me" tears and releasing tears. It is very easy to be stuck in "poor me" mode where abuse is concerned. No matter how much pain is felt or tears shed, it does not reduce the amount of hurt inside, it is simply recycled. It is important to make the distinction between releasing and wallowing. The victim often gets a great deal of satisfaction in bemoaning the pain rather than letting go of it. We know the difference between these two modes because releasing tears are often short lived and we feel better after shedding them. Victim tears can go on for a great deal of time and often it is only exhaustion that puts a stop to them. We do not feel better but heavy and burdened.

Fear of being hurt will play a very destructive and limiting role in most areas of our lives. It keeps us hidden behind our protective wall, not going into relationships or for jobs in case we are rejected. It stops us from being trusting and open with people in case they betray or hurt us. This will be particularly strong when abuse has occurred and many people live small, low grade lives as a result.

It is essential to process and remove the pain of abuse that is stored inside. This is a gradual process, it won't all come out at once. We can learn to welcome events that bring our pain to the surface rather than trying to avoid them.

FEAR

Once abuse has taken place, fear is going to play a large part in the life of the victim. My definition of fear is that it is a projection into the future of something that has already happened in the past. We often feel the greatest amount of fear once the danger has passed. This is certainly true within the arena of abuse. Our fear is often greater once the abuse has ended. We try to safeguard ourselves against anyone invading or hurting us again. It is a bit like shutting the stable door after the horse has bolted.

We may also find things and people to focus our fear on that are not really any threat to us. All the ways in which fear manifests itself as a result of abuse will devalue our lives to a great extent. I will address some of the more prominent fears.

Fear of intimacy is a powerful one. We build a wall around us as a protection from being hurt further. Not only do we not allow lovers or partners to get close but it shuts out friends and family as well. We may convince ourselves that we are safe with that wall around us but we also shut out love, affection, joy, fun and abundance. We may end up being hurt because people reject us or are put off by the wall. We may be lonely and think that people avoid us because we are unacceptable rather than that they are daunted by the wall.

When we are afraid, we try to create a safe space for ourselves. In order to do this, we may have to make our world so small that there is no room for growth. We may stay in a great deal, do a job that is not challenging or some people become agoraphobic and choose not to go out at all. Everything in our outer world becomes frightening. This is an existence and not a life.

Some people who have been abused are afraid of being visible or seen. They may wear black or dull colours and do nothing to make the most of their appearance in case it attracts unwanted attention onto them. This does little to boost their self-esteem and may result in them getting a negative response from people.

There may be a fear of authority. Sometimes we have an automatic reaction of giving our power away to people who are in a position of power or we may avoid them as much as possible.

Whatever each individual's lists of fear are, they will create great limitation. Many parts of life become off limits and no go areas. The fact is that when those fears were created, we were children and to an extent powerless in the situations. As adults we live in a grown up world where we are the authors of our own destinies. Whatever choices we make will manifest the reality that we want to create. If we choose to stay stuck in our fears, we will simply attract to us the very things that we are trying to avoid. All our fears no longer apply to us and consequently they are illusions. By dispelling these illusions and seeing that we now have the tools to handle anything that the world may throw at us, we can release ourselves from our fears once and for all.

EMOTIONAL SHUTDOWN

The emotions around sexual abuse are so strong and powerful that if they are not channelled safely, they can become a huge problem. We have already seen that many people turn these emotions against themselves. There is another pattern that many people employ to protect themselves from these emotions, they shut down.

Emotional shutdown can be extremely destructive. When we are numb to our own emotions, we lose touch with humanity and reality. I would say that every person who goes on to abuse other children is in a state of emotional shutdown. It would be inconceivable that anyone who is in touch with the emotions engendered by their own abuse could inflict them upon another living soul let alone an innocent child. This is one of the reasons why abusers rarely feel guilt for what they have done, they have disconnected with it along with their other emotions.

Emotional shutdown has many negative consequences. When we shut out our feelings like hurt, shame and anger, we also have to disconnect from the positive ones like love, joy, compassion and enthusiasm. We live a very limited existence if we don't let these things into our lives.

When we are not in touch with our own feelings, we are also disconnected from other people's; we are not aware of how we affect other people. Their emotions leave us cold. This is particularly difficult for the spouses and children of these people. They will certainly not get their emotional needs met by that person and a great deal of damage is created by it.

Emotional shutdown is mainly displayed by the male of the species. I honestly think that it probably lies at the source of virtually every destructive pattern of behaviour that is threatening to destroy our society. We can see it in teenage boys who go on the rampage, get into gangs, burgle or destroy property. It is behind ALL forms of abuse, it is behind bullying in schools, it is to be found in drug and alcohol problems, the drug being the means of shutdown. It is probably behind most divorces or failed relationships. On a more global scale, we can see this pattern in terrorism or when a country or government seeks to invade or destroy another one. Anyone in touch with their emotions could not contemplate inflicting that amount of pain on anyone else.

When we shut down from emotions, our biggest fear is to be reconnected with them. We therefore have to find ways to prevent this from happening. Most men will do this through their work. Whenever I see a workaholic, I know this person will be running away from their feelings. It cuts down the amount of time spent with the family who are quite likely to be strongly into their emotions. Computers and computer games are a godsend to those shutdown from their emotions. They can engage with a machine, feel powerful and in control. Many men prefer to communicate through e-mails or texting because there is little risk of being emotionally drawn in. Television and videos are also good distractions from emotions particularly if sport or action dramas are involved. Indeed, I think one of the reasons why so much violence on television and in films is tolerated is because the people who watch them are totally disconnected from their feelings and are not offended by them.

I think that if we are going to heal the world of all its many problems, reconnecting people with their feelings and releasing them has got to be a part of this. It should be introduced into programs in schools, in prisons, young offender units, drug rehabilitation centres and in relationship training.

When it is clear that a child has shut down emotionally, this is an indication that all is not well in their world. The signs could be spotted and the issues dealt with before they have a chance to fester and become a real problem.

AREAS AFFECTED BY ABUSE

WEIGHT

I would say that the majority of people I see who have been sexually abused have weight issues. Most of these are overweight but some are underweight or even anorexic as a result. There are many different reasons for this and most of them are unconscious.

Our bodies are designed to help us survive through all eventualities. When we perceive ourselves to be unsafe or under attack, the body will try to protect us. This occurs regardless of whether the attack is physical, sexual, emotional or mental. The best way the body knows to protect us is by putting on weight. This provides a physical buffer between our vital organs and the source of the danger. This protection will usually stay there until we feel safe and no longer vulnerable. It is very common to see people put on weight after a trauma and this is may be an indication in children that all is not well. Many people tell me that before their abuse they were skinny kids but the weight piled on during and after the abuse and they have never been able to lose it. The fact is that while we feel unsafe our bodies will try to help us out by putting on this suit of armour. Sadly, this can cause more problems than it solves as the weight makes us feel bad, unattractive and unacceptable in society. We have to get the message through to the body that we are safe and in control and are able to deal with situations without its help. If we don't do this, even if we lose the weight, it will be put back very quickly. I had a client who had been abused and managed to lose weight but she felt very unsafe and vulnerable at the lower weight and was happy to put it back on. She had not yet dealt with her abuse and her body reflected that.

Another reason why we may unconsciously put on weight as a result of sexual abuse is that we do not want to appear sexual. We may think that the abuse is to do with sex and that we attracted it to us because of how we looked. The understanding also works for those who are underweight. They become more androgynous and have fewer curves to attract attention. They may feel safe in their asexuality. When we are under or overweight our sex drive is reduced and this too may make us feel safe from unwanted attention. However, when these things occur when we are in a committed relationship, it can cause huge problems.

Weight is one of the ways that we self-abuse. We become tyrannised by food, both the having of it as well as the deprivation of it through fad diets and abstention. Every time we eat something, we beat ourselves up, feel guilty and then go back and have some more and so the cycle goes on. Food is no longer nurturing, it becomes a weapon and a battleground where whatever the outcome we are the loser. Foods like chocolate may become an addiction. There is often a huge emptiness inside caused by the abuse and food may seem to fill it momentarily. Some people have to feel full all the time or they are uncomfortable. Others will feel bad every time they are full as this will be a testament to their lack of will power and failure.

Food can also seem to act as a protection against our emotions. We have already seen that many powerful negative emotions are created out of abuse. Whenever these feelings begin to surface, we look for something to push them down again. Food may seem to fit the bill. It distracts us from what we are feeling. Many people admit that they are emotional eaters. They eat if they are angry, upset, lonely or frustrated. However, once again this is a self-defeating exercise because it often ends up creating more negative feelings than it offsets. When we have eaten, there is often a response of guilt, anger and self- disgust that may send the person straight back to the biscuit tin or the chocolate. This cycle then repeats again and again producing more self-destructive emotions.

We could use this pattern with food to heal some of the emotional aspects of the abuse. To do this takes awareness and discipline. First of all, we need to be conscious of when the pattern is taking place. For many people it is so ingrained that they complete the whole cycle without even realising it. It will also be very familiar since it has probably been reinforced daily. The discipline needed is to catch ourselves before we reach out for the food. We can then find out what the emotion is and what has triggered it. Once we allow the feeling to come to the surface, we are able to release it. At this point we can ask whether the food is still wanted. This process will be given in Part Two.

In healing abuse issues, it will be necessary to create a healthy attitude to both food and the physical body. Many people who have been abused completely detach from their physical bodies. It is as if it does not belong to them. This may well have been a protective mechanism created during actual times of abuse. However, if that detachment is there, our physical body may try to get our attention in order to become whole again. What better way to do this than by getting bigger and bigger or creating uncomfortable or painful ailments in the body. When the healing is done, the body no longer needs to grab our attention in such a way.

Learning to love the body with all its imperfections is one of the hardest things to do in life. Loving a body that has been the focus of abuse is going to be that much harder but it is essential to love and accept who and what we are, just as we are, if we are to break free from the legacy of abuse.

SEX

Sexual abuse affects each individual quite differently. One area that is virtually always influenced is quite understandably sex. However, there is a huge diversity in people's response to sex.

For all of us, our early sexual experiences will set the patterns for our sex lives later on. When the first introduction to sex is part of a loving relationship, this can be positive. But when it is abuse that forms this pattern, the results may be quite warped. It may be hard to associate sex with love, respect and commitment. Sex may become a power weapon to be wielded. Indeed, many people who have been abused get involved in the sex industry. This may be stripping or prostitution. The understanding is that they are now in control of it and they may enjoy the power and effect they have over their clients. There is no intimacy or emotions involved in these encounters and they can often despise or punish the men who are a stand in for their abusers. There is also the added bonus of getting well paid for their efforts.

There is a natural sexual boundary that we all have that seems to be broken down by sexual abuse. Children are sexually aware long before they would normally be. Consequently, it is not unusual for sexually abused children to start having consensual sex at a much earlier age than their contemporaries. This is often as young as twelve years old. There may also be a pattern of promiscuity and casual sex. Once again, the child will be trying to take control and use the power that their sexuality appears to give them.

For other people the effects of sexual abuse will be the total opposite. They may completely shut down sexually, not giving out any signals or sexual energy. This may be conscious or unconscious. If it is unconscious, the person may wonder why they are so unattractive to any potential partners, little realising that they are the creators of this state of affairs. Most of our communication is non-verbal, it is an energy or vibration that we give out and read about each other. If a person gets the message that someone is off limits, they do not bother to pursue them and face rejection. The fact is that most of us are hoping to find someone who will knock down our defenses, swim the crocodile infested moat, climb the highest mountain in order to win our favours. Sadly, the fairy tale does not play out in real life and if we want to be in a relationship we have to put out the right signals. Fear of abuse may prevent us from doing that.

Some people will fluctuate between the shut down and promiscuous modes. This gives very mixed signals and may prove confusing to both themselves and their partners.

Issues around sex will also show themselves in long term partnerships. This may not be evident in the early phases of the relationship but often emerges as damage from the past begins to surface, as inevitably it does. If any aspect of the abuse shows itself, like feeling used, disrespected, controlled or bullied, the person may well respond by shutting down sexually. This in effect pushes the partner away and creates feelings of rejection. They may ultimately begin to look outside the relationship for their sexual fulfilment. Having children is often a trigger for this whole cycle to emerge.

Sexual abuse often raises great confusion about sexual orientation. If a boy's first sexual experience is with a man, then he may question whether he is homosexual or not. Some women see men as being aggressors or unloving and may choose to be in sexual relationships with other women rather than men. This can cause a great deal of pain, particularly in families and societies that frown upon same sex relationships. Some people never come to terms with this and choose to abstain from any relationship altogether, rather than face up to an unwanted reality.

It may be necessary to work through sexual issues with an understanding partner, making it clear that any problems that arise are due to the abuse and are not personal to them.

RELATIONSHIPS

Relationships probably pay the highest price for abuse in childhood. In most other areas of life we are able to maintain our adult facade mode. Within a relationship we engage with the emotions, which will tap us into the child aspect and here lurks the damage. Very few relationships will be unaffected by abuse issues. However, the patterns may be very different depending on how each individual reacts to the abuse.

Some people simply perpetuate the whole pattern of abuse by choosing a partner who is controlling or even abusive. They may be a total doormat, unable to stand up for themselves or to say no to the things that they do not want. This is mainly a female pattern and these women stay in the destructive relationship because life has taught them not to expect any more than that. A controlling or abusive man will constantly be putting his partner down, belittling everything she does and is. When she hears these insults often enough, she will believe them. In these situations the controller is merely projecting his inadequacy onto her and will often accuse her of the very things that he is guilty of. It takes a great deal of help and support for a woman to remove herself from such a relationship.

Many people go to the opposite extreme of this and become very controlling in relationships as a result of abuse. They may believe that as long as they are in the driver's seat, they will not be hurt again. This ploy fails dismally. Not only do they create hurt for themselves by alienating people who love them but they cause untold hurt and damage to their families, passing the pattern and legacy on.

For a relationship to work optimally, we have to let our partner get close to us and admit them into the most intimate and vulnerable part of us. When we have been abused or hurt in the past, we usually shut this part of us off. We may even put a tough shell around it to protect us and keep any potential marauders out. The result of this is that no one is able to get near enough to discover the wonderful person behind the shell. Many people will be put off by the prickly, aggressive toughness and give us a wide berth. In healing this pattern it is essential that we see that we are able to protect ourselves from the people who may mean us harm and that we can remain open and available to those who are worthy of being our friends and lovers. To do this, we need to have the tools required but we also need to develop and utilise our greatest asset, our intuition. The intuition is able to see past the charm and facades people use to fool us and will tell us who to trust and who to avoid. This means we can move through life fearlessly and keep ourselves open.

There is an unhealthy pattern within relationships that has been born out of the many myths and fairy tales we were fed as children. Most of us are looking to be rescued and we see the person who is to do this to be our life partner. Consequently, we look to that person to make right everything that was not good or happy for us in childhood. In the early or "in love" phase of a relationship they appear to be able to do this. The state of love that we find ourselves in transcends all pain, fear, anger and difficulties. We think that our partner has done this and rescued us from the bondage of our damage. This is of course an illusion. When we begin to come down from this state, we tap back into all of our feelings and issues. We may then blame our partners for letting us down and not rescuing us. When there is abuse in the past, the need for rescue will be that much greater and so will the expectations that are projected onto the partner. The fact is **NO ONE OTHER THAN OURSELVES CAN RESCUE US**. Once this demand is taken off our partners, we stand a much more realistic chance of making the relationship work.

Another legacy of abuse in relationships is that many people do not find it easy to get into relationships. This may be a conscious decision on their part and that is fine. However, there are many individuals who are desperate to be in a relationship and yet find it very difficult to attract anyone to them. They may put this down to any number of things; they are not attractive enough, not clever enough, not successful enough, etc. None of these things are true. The fact is that there is a very strong unconscious pattern at work here. My definition of it is **WHEN WE ARE NOT IN A RELATIONSHIP AND WANT TO BE, IT IS BECAUSE**

OUR FEAR OF BEING HURT IS STRONGER THAN OUR DESIRE TO GET OUR NEEDS MET. This pattern is particularly strong in abuse cases because there will be a great deal of hurt and pain still figuring and a fear is always created out of our past experiences. From this definition we can see that if we want to change this pattern and attract someone into our lives, we have to reduce the fear/need ratio. To do this we have to release the hurt and pain and choose to perceive the situation differently.

There are many ways in which abuse affects relationships. The main thing that is needed is an awareness of whether the situation is about something that needs working on in the relationship or whether it is damage from the past coming in and being projected onto the partner.

SELF-ESTEEM

Probably the greatest casualty in any form of abuse is going to be our self-esteem, self-worth and self confidence. This will have a destructive knock-on effect on most other areas of life.

THE VALUE THAT WE GIVE TO OURSELVES WILL BE MIRRORED BACK TO US BY WHAT WE GET FROM THE WORLD. The fact is that we are the authors of our lives and we decide what we do and do not deserve. We are usually completely unaware that we are so powerful that we can create our reality in such a way. Sadly, most of what we do draw into our lives is not positive. Our level of self-esteem is the thing that determines where on the positive/negative spectrum we fall. The good news is that we can work on ourselves to raise that self-esteem and draw positive things and people into our lives.

When our self-esteem is very low, we tend to become passive and allow things to happen to us rather than make what we want happen. This will usually reinforce our victim mentality and the things we attract will usually be destructive. Our self-esteem will also determine the level of behaviour we will put up with from others. When this level is low, we will take a great deal. However, the moment anyone goes beyond that level, we draw the line. We may dissolve a relationship or resign from a job with an abusive boss. The line is very clearly defined but unconscious. An outside observer who has much higher self-esteem will be shocked to observe how someone at a lower level allows themselves to be treated. In effect our self-esteem denotes where we put our boundaries with people. It is human nature for people to take advantage and keep pushing until a boundary is reached. People who are on the take have a built in radar to locate those who are an easy touch and can be taken advantage of. These are always people with low self-esteem who have lax boundaries and cannot say no. This is how we allow people to continue to abuse us, thus reinforcing the negative beliefs we have about ourselves.

One area that will be detrimentally affected by low self-worth is money. This may emerge in a variety of ways. We may only ever consider ourselves worthy of low paid or menial jobs, not even trying to apply for anything that would provide abundance or fulfilment. Many women with low self-worth find themselves in relationships where the money is controlled by their partners and they are unable to do or buy what they want even if the money is there. They may find that money has hefty conditions attached that they are not willing to buy into.

Money can be a wonderful barometer as to our sense of worth. Strangely this is not decided by the amount we have but our reaction to it. People with vast amounts of money may have low self-worth. They may be amassing money and material possessions in order to compensate for their negative feelings about themselves but no matter how much they have, it is never enough. Our self-worth is high when we know that we have more than enough for our needs and desires. For some people this will be simple and modest, while others may choose a more opulent lifestyle. The degree to which we perceive ourselves to be lacking in anything will show our level of self-worth.

It is very clear how all kinds of abuse will erode our self-esteem to a very low level. When we are children we think that the world revolves around us, therefore anything that happens in our world must be down to us. Children take onto themselves the issues that they encounter in the family and shoulder the burden for things they had nothing what soever to do with. Abuse takes this pattern to the furthest degree. They are often completely mystified as to what they have done to deserve such treatment but in their understanding it must be their fault. Our self-esteem is usually set for life by how we are treated and what other people tell us about ourselves in childhood. Where there is abuse, this is going to leave a very poor impression. This is an illusion. Our treatment is totally down to the abuser and his or her issues, it is not a reflection in any way of who or what we are or what we deserve. This message has to be got across to the child within, if this pattern and its devastating legacy are to be healed.

As any healing takes place, this will reflect back on our self-esteem, we will see good things happen, positive and supportive people emerge and we do not put up with any crap from anyone. I find that when this occurs, our friends and family change in their attitude as we do or they ship out to pastures new. Either option being a positive!

METHODS OF SELF-ABUSE

We have seen that abusing the self is a very prevalent pattern where there is abuse. To the outside world much of this will not be apparent. We become very adept at hiding our damage and putting on a very good face externally. I am addressing in detail some of the ways in which we continue the pattern of abuse by projecting it onto ourselves. Many people will be able to associate with more than one of these.

FOOD

We have already looked at the issue of weight within abuse patterns. Food is probably the most common way in which we self-abuse. The issue here can be very confusing because while food may be the weapon of abuse, it is also our most important source of nurture.

What we are dealing with here are various forms of addiction. We use the substance to fill the emptiness and void inside created by giving our power away and disconnecting from our true inner Divine selves. With any addiction there will be momentary feelings of the substance fulfiling the brief and we may feel better. This is short lived and sets up a craving to have more of the substance in order to recreate the good feeling. After a while we no longer get the good feeling but we keep taking the substance in order to avoid devastating and painful withdrawal symptoms. This is the pattern within all addictions.

The solution to removing the physical aspects of an addiction is to cut down the amount taken gradually over time and then facing the period of withdrawal by going cold turkey. Once the substance is out of the system, the cravings will decrease. This may be applied to many addictions but it is hard to apply to food because we need it in order to survive.

Most of the food addictions involve things like chocolate, sugar, wheat and junk or refined foods. These are usually the foods people choose to put a buffer between them and their feelings. They are also the foods that will put on the most weight. If the addiction is there, we may need to view these foods as we would alcohol or drugs in applying the solution. If there is a craving there is also an addiction.

We can use food to tyrannise ourselves in many different ways. When we overeat we beat ourselves up for our looks or lack of will power. When we become anorexic, we punish ourselves with our hunger, our unhealthiness or for every morsel that we eat. Bulimia creates a pattern of binging and purging which combines both of these and does untold damage to the physical body.

Many people admit to what is known as comfort eating. They look to food to be their friend and to distract them from whatever is not working in their lives. Most comfort eating actually creates a good deal of discomfort. We do not feel good in our bodies, we are bloated and our clothes do not fit. Comfort eating can become a deeply entrenched pattern that we have to break. We may need to learn to be in the discomfort of the situation and work through the issues rather than turning to food to distract us from them.

CIGARETTES

Cigarettes are another common addiction that will often play a part in abuse issues. Cigarettes give the illusion of providing a buffer between us and our feelings. While the effects of the cigarette last it will seem to achieve this as well as feeding the physical addiction. It will calm us down or give us a high or feelings of pleasure. Once the effect wears off quite the reverse occurs. There may be feelings of fear or anxiety and a great deal of anger may surface. The cigarette does not create these feelings, it merely liberates them from their storage facility.

When there has been abuse there is going to be an excess of emotions like fear and anger and we might want to avoid feeling them. The cigarette is a double edged sword. It may represent the friend and protector but it is also the enemy.

Everyone knows how damaging smoking is to our health. The cancers caused by smoking can be particularly nasty and hard to cure. This knowledge does not stop many people from doing the thing that is guaranteed to shorten their lives and create a great deal of pain and suffering in the process.

Many people who give up smoking return to it because they cannot handle the feelings that emerge during the withdrawal process.

DRUGS

When we talk about a drug problem, the image that usually comes to mind is of a heroin or cocaine addiction. While undoubtedly many victims of sexual abuse may go this route to blot out the pain of their suffering, this is by no means the biggest problem. Far greater is the number of people who are addicted to prescription drugs.

Many people who have been abused will suffer from depression or panic or anxiety attacks. When they go to a doctor complaining of these conditions, they will usually be given anti-depressants or tranquillisers. These pills will often mask the symptoms or feelings in the short term but many are very addictive and the withdrawal symptoms can be far worse than the original symptoms they were there to deal with. We are not aware of how many people this is affecting because they may appear to be perfectly normal on the outside in their everyday lives. Only they will know how they feel inside, they may feel detached from what is going on around them. This is a form of emotional shutdown and once again it shuts out the good feelings with the bad, leaving people in an emotional no man's land.

A life spent in the grip of drugs whether recreational or prescription is a life wasted. It takes huge strength of character to rescue oneself from this tyranny. Many people who have been abused are in so much emotional distress that they do not want to live and certain drugs provide the oblivion that they are craving. Indeed, for some death would be a welcome release from the pain.

We can begin to see a pattern emerging within the methods people use to self-abuse. There are certainly self-destructive elements in all the methods chosen.

However, the overriding motivation seems to be to find something to block out the pain and the emotions associated with the abuse.

ALCOHOL

There are two types of alcoholics. I call these genetic alcoholics and circumstantial alcoholics. There is no doubt that there is a genetic predisposition to drink and not to be able to stop when they have had enough but we are not concerned with that form of alcoholism.

Circumstantial alcoholics will drink in response to situations in their outer world that are beyond their control. This may be things like the death of a loved one, divorce, redundancy, homelessness or many other things. As with other substances, the alcohol provides a buffer between us and our emotions. Where there is sexual abuse, some people may turn to alcohol as early as in their teens and it becomes a crutch from that point on.

Like many means that we use to protect ourselves, alcohol will backfire usually on us. The first few drinks may well be pleasurable and numb us from our feelings. However, there comes a point where alcohol may do the very opposite. The drinker may become very morose or aggressive when this line has been stepped over, thus creating the very situation that they were seeking to avoid.

As with other addictions, the pain of withdrawal is often enough to keep us taking the destructive substance. When the withdrawal takes place, we are often faced with the very emotions that we were using the alcohol to run away from.

Children of alcoholics will admit that their lives have been totally blighted by their parents' drinking. This is another way in which the legacy of abuse can be passed on down through the generations and it can be every bit as destructive as the abuse itself.

SELF HARMING

This is a pattern of behaviour that does not receive a huge amount of publicity but it is very prevalent in abuse victims. There may be a great deal of shame attached to this activity because it may seem to indicate mental imbalance.

The motivation in self harming is once again to alleviate emotional pain. The understanding is that when we are in physical pain, it supersedes any emotional pain and some much needed relief from the negative feelings is provided. This shows how intolerable the emotions are if it is preferable to feel physical pain.

The means by which the pain is inflicted may vary but common methods are cutting usually with razors, burning or digging the fingernails into the flesh until it bleeds. The evidence of these wounds must be hidden so people often wear clothes with long sleeves even in mid summer.

This form of self-abuse is as much an addiction as all the other methods I have highlighted. There will be a desire and craving to do the cutting and there will be initial good feelings associated with the action. This will then be followed by a low and possibly feelings of guilt and shame but there will also be a need to repeat the wounding. Just because there is not a chemical substance involved does not make this behaviour any less addictive.

SELF-BULLYING

One of the most potent ways in which we can abuse ourselves is by bullying. Here the pattern of abuse is perpetuated as we are both the abuser and the victim. This will be done on many different levels and in different ways. We will probably berate ourselves within our mind talk. We will call ourselves names, tell ourselves that we are stupid, useless, ugly, a loser and many more. We will be far more vicious to ourselves than anyone in our outer world could ever be. This inner dialogue may take place during all our waking hours. It has probably been there so long that we do not see it as anything out of the ordinary.

When this bullying occurs, it is the adult aspect of ourselves heaping the abuse on the inner child. This child within already believes that it deserves to be ill-treated and is unworthy of any love, support, or nurture and we simply reinforce this belief time after time.

Within this pattern, we may further enforce the bullying by allowing other people to carry on the bullying where we leave off. This may be a partner, boss or friend that we give this permission to, We don't question their right to use or take advantage of us.

Another way in which we can bully ourselves is by the choices we make. Everyday we are being faced with choices and it may be clear that one option will create a situation that would give us joy or pleasure and the other choice the opposite. When we are being self-abusive, we may bully ourselves into choosing the negative option. We may even feel compelled to always create the worst possible scenario instead of the best.

We need to become aware of how we treat ourselves, what our mind talk is saying and when we are not nurturing ourselves. We can choose not to be the bully and self-destructive, we can start to love and protect the poor abused child within instead of being its worst enemy.

One thing is certain and that is that we cannot heal the adult until we have healed the child and to do this we have to put a stop to being part of the problem instead of the solution.

VICTIM AND TYRANT

Within abuse it seems that there are only two possible roles that we can play; that of victim or tyrant. Many people choose to stay a victim while others will alternate between the two extremes.

I will look at both these dynamics in detail. First, the victim. Anybody who has been abused will have felt like a victim but this mentality lasts far longer than the abuse itself. When we are victims, we believe ourselves to be powerless and therefore unable to stop or prevent what is happening to us. Victims will tend to be very passive, allowing other people to make their choices for them rather than making any decisions for themselves. When we are victims, we do not take responsibility for ourselves, we hand that over to anyone who is willing to take it on.

The victim mode creates an imprint that is like a magnet to negativity. Any bad luck will appear to be irresistibly drawn to them. I myself find that when I am in the presence of a victim that I am much more impatient and quick to be irritated by them than I would normally be and I have to make an effort to quell these feelings. I realise that if I have this reaction to them, most other people will too and many will disguise it less. Victims often go from one drama to another and can become addicted to the attention that the dramas give them. This addiction will often play a large part in them not wanting to give up their victimhood.

Many people cling to being a victim for dear life, they may define themselves based on all the terrible things that have happened to them in the past. In working with people I find it most difficult to help people who are stuck in victim mode. I find that if I am putting more energy into their healing than they are then this is a clear indication that they are not willing to move on. It is only when we commit ourselves to giving up this very destructive illusion that we will allow ourselves to be healed. We can throw a life belt to drowning victims but if they do not choose to cling on nothing can be done.

Victims will tend to drain a great deal of energy from the people around them. A clear sign that someone is stuck in this mode is that we feel tired or wiped out after spending a short period of time with them. This is called "the psychic vampire syndrome." People who live with psychic vampires are often ill as their life force energy is being taken from them on a constant basis. This energy seems to go into a black hole, never to be seen again. Victims can also be very needy, expecting everyone else to fulfil their needs rather than doing it themselves.

There are degrees of victimhood. I have been describing what is probably the extreme of this. Most of us will have some aspects of the victim within us but this will often be tempered with more positive sides to our nature.

The tyrant is obviously at the opposite end of the spectrum. Where the victim works with negative female energy, the tyrant works with negative male energy. While the victim is internalised the tyrant will be very evident in the outside world. A tyrant works on the theory "get them before they get you." They will often be bullies and control freaks and they will almost certainly be in a state of emotional shutdown. They will rarely have any remorse for the pain they inflict on other people.

Ironically, tyrants may be quite successful in their chosen field, being highly motivated and driven toward success. They may be high rollers who live on the edge a great deal and they may fall as quickly as they rise.

Naturally tyrants make appalling spouses and parents. They will rule with fear and have to create a climate in which they are obeyed by those around them. They will aspire to positions of power both in the home and in the external world but this will always be ego power. In reality they will still feel powerless and a victim inside, hence the never ending quest for power.

Tyrants will despise weakness in any form as this will remind them of their own vulnerability that they are trying to disguise. Having said this, tyrants and victims make very comfortable bed fellows and will tend to attract each other. A victim will put up with a tyrant where others would not. It may seem odd to say it but a tyrant needs a victim in order to function.

I have demonstrated victims and tyrants in their most extreme forms. Most of us are a mixture of the two and will often alternate between them. We may be very careful to keep the victim hidden inside and appear to be strong and in control on the outside. However, for most of us the veneer is very thin. I always believe that the degree of hardness a person displays to the world is an indication of how much pain and vulnerability there is underneath. This was demonstrated to me when I was running a group. When I turned up one week there was a new lady there. She had a very forbidding expression on her face and she was chain smoking. I admit that I was very intimidated by her. She seemed to glare at everybody. A voice in my head reminded me "the harder the shell, the softer the inside." Sure enough, it turned out that she had been sexually abused by her father and brother and by the end of the session the shell had fallen away and she was crying like a baby.

I have already explained how we may use the tyrant aspect of us on the victim within us. We are displaying both sides at the same time but the whole pattern is internalised. Other people will be completely unaware of the abuse that is going on.

Both victims and tyrants are coming from a position of powerlessness. This may seem strange in the case of the tyrant. However, the more power we need to obtain from others, the less we actually have.

When there has been abuse or difficult circumstances in childhood, it may appear as if we only have two choices. For instance, if a child has seen its father hitting its mother constantly and the mother accepting this punishment without question. The child may then think that the only two options for it are either to be the one who beats or the one who is beaten. Sometimes this will be a totally unconscious decision. "If I don't want this to be done to me then I have to be the one to do it." This of course perpetuates these destructive family patterns that pass down through the generations.

However, there is always a third option and this is the one we need to take in order to break these cycles of abuse.

The third option says; "I know how it feels to be abused and powerless and I don't want to repeat that experience, nor would I want to inflict it upon anyone else knowing how awful it is. I therefore choose to grow and learn through this experience and heal myself and use what I know to help others and make the world a better, safer place as a result." It is only by choosing the third option that we can stop the rot. Within the third option we take our personal power back and use it to empower others to heal the damage.

We can apply the third option to any area of life and the beauty of it is that everyone wins, there are no losers. The third option is the phoenix rising from the ashes, transformation through adversity and it is available to absolutely everyone. For many people it may simply be a matter of knowing that the third option exists and that they only have to choose it for themselves.

SACRIFICE

There is a very strong pattern that virtually everyone plays out in some shape or form. This will usually start under the age of five but will take hold and often continue right through our lives. This pattern is sacrifice.

Small children are aware of a great deal more than we give them credit for. They can tune into the feelings and thoughts of their families. This is a gift that often diminishes with time. We have an overriding need to save the family and most particularly our parents.

The methods of sacrifice used are many and varied and some would not be recognised as such. Many children take on their parents emotions in the mistaken assumption that they are taking them off their parents and relieving them of the burden. What is happening in reality is that there are now two people feeling the emotions instead of just one, thus doubling the amount of emotion. One of the most frequent incarnations of sacrifice is being the good girl or boy. Here we sacrifice our own needs and the natural expression of our emotions in order not to add to the problems within the family. This may happen when another child is difficult or demanding and we see the toll that this takes on our parents.

At the other end of the spectrum some children might allow themselves to be made the scapegoat, allowing the negative emotions within the family to be dumped on them. The understanding here is that if they are taking the brunt of the negativity then other members of the family are being spared it.

There are huge issues of sacrifice played out within the arena of sexual abuse. Some children allow the abuse to continue rather than speak up because they are aware of the devastating effect it will have on the family. Sometimes an older sibling may let the abuse take place thinking that its younger siblings would be spared as a result. When they find out later that the younger ones were being abused as well, there is often a great deal of anger. This pattern of sacrifice and protection will often extend into adulthood. The code of silence to protect the ones we love from having to face reality is very strong and many people would not dream of breaking it. This is why the full extent of the problem is not truly known.

VULNERABILITY

Vulnerability is a very misunderstood commodity and yet it is essential to our wholeness as a human being. I believe that vulnerability is a very powerful force for good and that if we use it positively, the world would be a far better place.

Sadly, vulnerability has come to be seen in a negative way. It represents weakness, the victim, pain and fear, being at a disadvantage and open to attack. Consequently, we are at great pains to bury, hide or protect our vulnerability so that no one can see it and use it against us.

In reality vulnerability is an invitation to love and nurture. When someone allows themselves to be genuinely vulnerable,(this is not being needy or a victim) we open our hearts to them, we see their loveliness and innocence shining through and we will probably go to great lengths to help and support that person.

An alarming dynamic has arisen within our society and this involves emotional shutdown. The main reason that people disconnect from their emotions is to remove themselves from their vulnerability. As a result of this they try to destroy anyone who is displaying any vulnerability as this might tap them back into their own. This then sends out the message that if we show our vulnerability, we will be attacked, this leads others to shut down or find ways to hide or disguise their vulnerability. I cannot stress just how destructive this pattern is.

We have here a lose-lose situation because we appear to be open to attack from certain quarters if we allow ourselves to show our vulnerability and yet when we protect and defend ourselves, we invite attack. We become an army in search of a war. This needs to be turned around and a win-win situation put in its place.

The biggest casualty of this dynamic is probably relationships. I believe vulnerability to be one of the most essential ingredients needed for a successful relationship. It invites genuine love, openness, trust, acceptance, caring and understanding. Most relationships fail because we shut these parts of us away and do not give access to them. Animals and children who have not yet shut down are so easy to love because their vulnerability shines out and we (those that are not shut down) open our hearts to them.

The Course in Miracles states that our safety lies in our defencelessness. I think this refers to our vulnerability. If we do not seek to defend it and remain open, we are truly safe. This would only not be true if we gave someone the power to hurt or destroy us. This is a choice we can decide not to make.

I believe the quality that made people like Marilyn Monroe, Princess Diana and Audrey Hepburn world icons, is vulnerability. It is very attractive and appealing, it draws people to us. Sadly, they also had a great deal of damage that took its toll on them.

Where there has been abuse, we will usually try to hide our vulnerability, believing that this was what drew the abuse to us in the first place. With any protection mechanism, we end up creating the very thing we are seeking to avoid. Our prickly, aggressive or tough outer shell lets people think that we don't have sensitive feelings and that they can do and say things that they would not dream of to a more delicate person. People mirror back to us the energy we are putting out, little realising that this is a smoke screen for our vulnerability.

Part of the healing of abuse will involve clearing out the pain and fear that has been locked in with the vulnerability and then dismantling the hard facade and allowing the wonderful vulnerable person to emerge. I promise you that this is a strength and not a weakness.

PHYSICAL ABUSE

I have very much concentrated on sexual abuse so far because I feel that it is a subject that is still taboo and is not sufficiently dealt with in therapeutic circles. However, the affects of other forms of abuse will be very similar. There will be a victim mentality, the emotions of anger, pain and fear and also beliefs that we must somehow deserve the abuse. It is also about power and control. Much that I have already covered in this book can be applied to any form of abuse and I would advise that the clearing exercises be used for all types.

Physical abuse in childhood is very common and is often not recognised as such. There is a very fine line between discipline and abuse and many people are not aware of when it has been crossed. Some parents will hide the need to abuse behind strict parenting. This is why moves to make smacking illegal gets my support because it is very difficult to protect children from this type of abuse. The issue becomes very confused when it is permissible to hit a child.

I will look at some of the patterns that seem to repeat within physical abuse. While it is mainly perpetrated by men this is by no means as predominant as it is in sexual abuse. Many mothers will physically abuse their children. There are also strong family patterns of physical abuse passing down through the generations. Obviously physical abuse is less covert than sexual abuse. It would be almost impossible to hide the actions or the resulting marks from other members of the family. This means that siblings or other parents have to turn a blind eye to the abuse in order for it to be able to continue. Often the level of fear in the whole family will ensure this. Other members may fear that the abuse will be heaped on them if they were to make a stand or question it. This will often create a sense that the non-abusive parent is in collusion. These parents will often even use the threat of the abusive parent as a means of getting obedience. Within these family patterns of physical abuse there will be a variety of different options. Sometimes a father may be physically abusing his wife and his children, other parents may just abuse the children, while other will just abuse the spouse. The latter pattern is every bit as destructive to the child.

Where there is abuse within the home, there is often a huge need to present a close family front to the outside world. They might be churchgoers or pillars of the community and greatly respected. It is often shocking to friends and neighbours when the truth comes out.

The legacy of physical abuse within the family often passes on in different ways. The children of abuse will usually make the unconscious decision as to whether to be the tyrant or the victim. Many women will get into a whole series of relationships where they are beaten or abused. It is as if the imprint is formed and they only attract and are attracted by potential abusers. I must stress that most of these men are very charming in the courtship phase of the relationship. It is only when a commitment has been made that the abuse begins.

Children will be affected by this pattern even if they only witnessed the abuse rather than having had it done to them. Our parents are our role models and if we think that the only two choices we have is to either be abused or to abuse them, we will plump for one of those options. Many children have been completely traumatised by watching one parent physically abuse the other.

Many child or spouse abusers may be perfectly lovely people for the majority of the time and their children will probably have a great deal of love for them. There is usually a set pattern and cycle of abuse that plays out time and again. Alcohol often plays a large part in this. Many victims describe a Jekyll and Hyde personality that emerges when the parent is drunk. It is as if they were spoiling for a fight and they don't care who they hit. Often there is a build up of tension caused by stress of difficulties, it feels like a pressure cooker building up and everyone is on tenterhooks waiting for it to blow. Afterwards there is often a time of remorse and peace within the house. The abuser may try to make up for what he has done.

It is quite common for one child to bear the brunt of the abuser's wrath. They become the scapegoat and other members of the family may encourage this as it keeps them out of the line of fire. When this occurs there is often a great deal of guilt attached to this and the victim will probably be in a state of sacrifice.

Since the abolition of corporal punishment the pattern of physical abuse in childhood is mainly contained within the direct family. Many people may still bear the emotional scars from canings and physical punishment at school. Thankfully this barbaric practice has all but been wiped out in the western world. There is very little physical abuse in the broader family or within the community. It would not be stood for and is illegal.

I will look in greater detail at the issue of physical abuse versus discipline. Where is this line drawn? I believe that when a parents hits a child or lashes out in anger, the line is crossed. When we are angry we lose touch with reality, we are not aware of how hard or where we are hitting, we are just looking for a target for our anger. Our anger will usually be out of proportion to the transgression committed and the child will sense and be frightened by the anger. I realise in having said this there are not many parents who have not hit or wanted to hit out in anger. This is not about blame, it is about bringing this awareness into being. I know that parents feel dreadful when they have hit in anger and will often apologise to the child as a result. When we know better, we do better.

Another form of punishment that I feel can be quite abusive is deferred physical punishment. A child may be told to go to their room and in a few hours someone will come and beat them. The fear built up in this time is far worse than the actual beatings. Some mothers do this, they defer the punishment until the father comes home and administers it.

Hitting or smacking is very common in certain cultures and it is not unusual to hear people say "I got beaten as a child and it never did me any harm." I would think that the majority of people who say this are in a state of emotional shutdown. They are disconnected from the harm that it did and they will usually be happy to pass this down to their own children.

Once again, the issues of power and control are very strong within physical abuse. They are simply bullies picking on those who are vulnerable. When I ask men who have been physically abused as children what put an end to it, they will usually tell me that they fought back. Sometimes it is only the threat of it that is enough, confirming the bully mentality. If we stand up to the bully they will back down as they are cowards at heart. Some men say that as soon as they were taller than their father, the abuse stopped. Many men equate physical size with power. This is totally untrue, there is no correlation between size and real power.

It is often quite hard to get people to admit to having been physically abused. The abuse will often be in response to something the child will have perceived that it did wrong. It will therefore believe that the punishment is justified. We may also try to protect our parents by not heaping any accusations on them. There is obviously a huge spectrum of physical abuse, most of us will have experienced incidents at the lower end of the scale. This does not mean we had bad parents. Every parent does their best with the knowledge and experience available to them.

Not all physical abuse involves hitting. Many children experience other forms of physical cruelty. It may be things like being locked in a room or cupboard, being deprived of food or being made to consume bad food or disgusting things. In extreme cases the child may be burnt with cigarettes, tied up or subjected to other forms of torture. There is often a warped or sick minded person doing these things and the truth may only come out if the child dies.

There is a lovely saying that it takes a whole village to bring up a child. In times gone by there was more of a community spirit and people would mind or look after each others' children. Families often consisted of three or more generations living in one house. In certain evolved cultures there would be a person whose role would be to spot if a child were not thriving and get to the bottom of what the problem was. Sadly, we now live very contained lives in small units and we are loath to interfere in other peoples' problems. When there have been well publicised cases of children who have died after prolonged physical and emotional abuse, neighbours and teachers admitted seeing the signs but not daring to do anything about it. Once again, we are afraid of the bully's wrath being turned on us.

The fact is that children are in most danger from their parents. The fear and emphasis on danger is put on the outside world but for many babies and children the least safe place for them is in the home. This also extends to siblings. Many children are abused by their brothers and sisters. Again it is hard to know where the line is drawn between boisterous horseplay and actual abuse. There are huge issues of jealousy and sibling rivalry that occur in most families. It is not unusual for older children to bully younger ones. However, there is a pattern that I have come across frequently with my clients. When a baby is born when the older child is between two and five years old, there can be dangerous feelings of jealousy toward the baby. Numerous clients have admitted to me that they tried to kill their baby brother or sister when they were small. Methods used may vary. Ones that I have come across are pushing a crawling baby down the stairs, off a chair, poking a wire into the eye and suffocation. These actions never take place when any adult is around and most parents will be blissfully unaware of what has taken place. I always advise parents **NEVER** to leave a baby or small child alone with an older sibling under the age of five. The children who do this are not bad or wicked, they are aware that what they are doing is wrong but they are responding to and acting upon their emotions, which is what small children do. They have not yet learned to rationalise, see the big picture or the consequences of their actions. This form of abuse can be safeguarded against as long as the awareness is there. These siblings are often close friends later on and laugh about the incident.

In virtually all cases of physical abuse the parent or sibling is projecting their anger, jealousy, frustration, fear or pain onto the child. It is all about the abuser and actually has nothing to do with the victim personally. They just happen to be there to catch the fall out. Most physically abused children will see this very differently. They will usually be aware that something that they have said or done will have provided the trigger for those feelings and therefore the subsequent abuse. They will believe it to be their fault and think that they must deserve the punishment that comes from this. People living in a house with an abusive person are always treading on eggshells. They never know what will set the person off. It is often harmless or innocuous things. Any subject that has set off an outburst in the past becomes off limits. Over time this does not leave much to talk about. They are always trying to second guess the abuser by saying or doing the things they want rather than being true to themselves.

The scars of physical abuse are much deeper than any that might be experienced on a body level. Self-esteem and confidence will be strongly affected here. Once we have been beaten in one sense, we will often allow life to continue to beat us up and when this is not happening we may beat ourselves up.

When there is physical abuse within a home, we learn very quickly to suppress our emotions as these will be likely to incite the abuser. This results in a build up of pent up emotions that are liable to explode when we are older, with possible negative consequences. Rage is anger out of control and we are all capable of killing or seriously hurting others in rage. It is essential that the emotions associated with abuse are processed in a safe and gentle way so that we do not endanger others with our feelings.

EMOTIONAL ABUSE

There are very few of us who can say that we did not receive any emotional abuse in our childhoods. However, there are hugely varying degrees of this and at the top end of the scale the devastation can be huge. Virtually all emotional abuse is born out of the damage sustained by the perpetrators as children.

Many people who have been emotionally abused believe that this is worse than physical abuse because the physical wounds heal. It feels like there is a legacy to emotional abuse that is a gaping wound inside that does not heal.

There are strong family patterns of emotional abuse. The imprint is to treat our children as we were treated and this takes many forms. Much emotional abuse could be averted simply by teaching parenting and making parents conscious and aware of how they might damage their children. No parent sets out to hurt or destroy their children. They do their best with the knowledge and resources they have. It therefore stands to reason that if they had more knowledge and greater resources, they would be able to do a better job. This should surely become a priority in the education system.

The most common form of emotional abuse is verbal. We are told that we are stupid, bad, ugly, useless, hopeless, a waste of space and countless other negatives. These adjectives may be put onto us on a constant basis. We have no choice but to believe it. Who we believe ourselves to be will have been put onto us by the age of five. It is very difficult to pull off these labels once they have been stuck on. I have often observed parents out in public with their children blasting them constantly with negativity and the poor little ones taking it all in. In every case this is a projection onto the child of the parents' thoughts and feelings about themselves and what they were told. A child's awareness of itself is then created out of the damage of the parent and so the cycle passes down to the next generation and so on.

Not only do parents dump their beliefs about themselves onto the children but they may also put their emotions onto them. Children may feel to blame for whatever is not working in the family. If there is something difficult like a divorce or bereavement in the family, the children often end up taking it on board and feeling responsible.

Probably the most destructive and abusive emotion that children deal with is their parents' anger. This often bursts out and while it may not result in physical abuse, the sheer power and negativity will create great fear in children. There is probably not a parent living who has not lost their temper and shouted at the kids on many occasions. Most parents feel dreadful when this occurs, they know that what they have done has caused pain. Nobody is perfect. Where this becomes a big problem is when it happens on a regular basis. The child may not appear to react or be affected on the outside but the wound goes deep. Things are often said in anger that are not meant or true but they cannot be retracted.

I would say that emotional abuse in the family is perpetrated equally by men and women. With the clients whom I see there is a pretty even spread of those who have issues with their mother and those whose father has been the source of the problems. I think the reason that there are more instances of women perpetrating this type of abuse than the other two forms, is that women are more in touch with their emotions. This will include some negative emotions. I think that within this pattern, women tend to project more onto their daughters than onto their sons. This may set up other issues of favouritism and unfairness. This pattern also works in reverse with men projecting more onto their sons. We have to remember here that the abuse is what has been put onto the parent being transferred to the child. The child who is most identifiable with the parent will tend to bear the brunt. For instance, if a father was the oldest child and he took the lion's share of his father's abuse, he will tend to repeat this pattern with his eldest son. The effect of unconscious patterning is huge. The child in question will notice the different treatment being given to their siblings but they will probably see this as proof that they are not good enough or that there is something wrong with them that they are being treated this way.

Emotional abuse can often take the form of an absence of emotions. One or both parents may be in a state of emotional shutdown. The child will not get any sense of being loved by that parent and may feel totally disconnected from it. As always the children will see this as a reflection of themselves rather than recognising the damage created within the parent. The pain that results from this situation is enormous and often lingers past the demise of that parent.

Where there is emotional abuse, the person creating it is often mentally unbalanced or ill. They will be very erratic in their behaviour, sometimes suffocatingly loving and at other times incredibly cruel. They are hugely unpredictable and the child will never know where it is with the parent. At a young age the child will have no understanding of the parent's problem and take full blame for any negative situations. There is often a huge amount of shame around mental illness. The child will not dare bring friends home and there is often a pact to protect the family or parent by not revealing what goes on in the home. I have had many clients who bear massive emotional scars from a mentally ill parent. This may be quite difficult to come to terms with. Some unstable people can be extremely vicious and cruel when they are in the throes of an episode. This is the illness and not them talking and when they are in a normal phase they will probably not remember what was said. The need to protect the mentally ill parent often means that members of the family have to suppress the enormous anger that they have for the parent. In effect they are seeing the parent in most danger from themselves. The suppression of anger may cause bouts of depression or the projection of the anger onto other safer targets, both of these being destructive.

An indirect form of emotional abuse is when parents fight and argue in front of the child. Very often there is more aggression in a verbal fight than there is in a physical one. Both parents will be saying things in anger that they do not mean or are not true. The child will feel powerless and helpless and have greatly divided loyalties. Children withdraw when they are constantly subjected to this kind of abuse. Many tell me that they would go to their rooms and turn up their music very loud to drown out the sound.

Others would need to be near to try and protect whichever parent is the most vulnerable. This form of abuse has a long-lasting effect. Many people are not able to tolerate raised voices and in their relationships will do anything to avoid an argument. This is often enough to incite their partner to become particularly angry, which in turn will create the very situation they are seeking to avoid.

Sometimes we think that the only way that we can be emotionally abused is by negative behaviour. It can be every bit as abusive to a child to give it too much power and allow it to have everything that it wants. There are no boundaries here and consequently the child will feel insecure and push the parents in an effort to find out where the boundaries lie. The child can then become the tyrant in the home and not feel good about itself. Huge resentment can also build up in the family against this child.

There can often be a great deal of emotional abuse perpetrated by siblings. Jealousy is a very powerful emotion and there is often a great deal of it in families. The jealousy is usually from the older siblings to the younger ones. Parents are often more relaxed and lenient with their younger children as they learn and grow through the pitfalls of parenting. There may also be more money available for younger children than when families first started out. For whatever reason and whether justified or not the means that jealousy displays itself will often be in emotional abuse. This may be limited to name calling or subtly ostracising the child but in some extreme cases it can result in years of cruelty and a calculated campaign of abuse. The sibling will probably feel that it is evening out the imbalance by creating misery in the child's life. Much of this will be done behind the parents' backs and the child soon learns that to tell means suffering more in the long run. Siblings tend to know each other's vulnerabilities and Achilles heels. This will then become the preferred area of abuse because it has the greatest impact. This form of long term systematic abuse is hugely damaging and will often continue way past childhood. It may create a family rift that is never healed. In these situations the child gives its power away to the older sibling and will tend to believe all the taunts that are heaped upon it. None of these will be true, they are simply illusions that have been bought into that have been repeated so often that they become reality. Part of the healing of this kind of abuse is to once again know that the issue or problem does not lie with the victim but with the perpetrator.

Many of my clients have suffered a great deal of emotional and mental abuse at the hands of their teachers. This is probably one of the few areas outside the home where this occurs. There are some cruel and sadistic teachers who take great delight in using their power over defenceless children. I am not for one moment suggesting that this is rife in every school but one teacher will impact upon hundreds of children over a career. The child never forgets the name of the abusive teacher. These people are bullies plain and simple. They pick on children who are vulnerable or stand out in the crowd. There is usually a pattern as to who gets picked on, this will often be a clue to the issue that the teacher is projecting onto the child. Just as with sexual abuse, the child will probably suffer in silence, not telling parents or challenging the school or teacher. This kind of bullying will often blight the whole of the child's education and these victims are rarely academically successful in this regime. I have had clients who were convinced that they were thick and stupid due to the behaviour of such teachers only to go to another school and find out that they were actually very bright. The low self-esteem created by this form of abuse is very hard to shake off and many people do not manage it.

Bullying within the peer group is the final area of emotional abuse that I am addressing. This is a big problem that needs a book of its own to cover it. All of the familiar issues of power and control are at work here. The most common forms of bullying are taunts and name calling. Sometimes it does extend into physical abuse. There are many instances of children committing suicide as a result of constant bullying. Schools do not want to deal with this issue and often try to brush it under the carpet. The bully will usually need a team of side kicks in order to be able to wield its power. These are often people who are afraid of the bully and see the only alternative to being bullied is to join in with the bully. They give their power to the bully just as the victims do and it is this that enables the bully to have its reign of terror. Take this away from bullies and they become completely powerless. If schools learned to completely isolate the bully in this way and diffusing the power dynamic, it would be a start. The fact is that many teachers are also intimidated by the bully and give their power to it as well. A bully will either have been bullied or controlled at home or at school or have come from a family that gives it too much power and not enough boundaries.

The effects of bullying last long into adulthood and may put people in a permanent victim mode. It is common to repeat this pattern as adults either in the family or in the work place. Many mothers get bullied by their children. Victims often find themselves recreating the school situation at work with either co-workers or their boss. They may even attract friends who are very controlling or use them.

We have to keep in mind that bullies are cowards at heart. They pick on people who are gentle, vulnerable and won't fight back. If we stand up to a bully, they back down and crumble. Sometimes the best way to view a bully is as the damaged victims that they are under their tough exterior. Give them compassion and not power and see their vulnerability emerge. There was a bully at my boarding school. She never bullied me but she did the weaker girls. She had a difficult home background, her mother had died and she was being brought up by a strict maiden aunt. She would often have nightmares and would come and sob on my bed when they occurred. Her bullying was just a big cover up for all the pain and misery that she had suffered. If we keep this understanding at the forefront of our minds when working with bullying issues, we can downgrade them from ogre to someone that we can feel sorrow and compassion for.

I believe that all the scars and wounds created by emotional and mental abuse can be healed. We have to change the beliefs and perceptions we took on at the time and begin to see it in a different light. There are many strong emotions like anger and pain that are the residue and these too need to be released and not passed on to others or used to bully ourselves with.

ACCEPTANCE

There are various states that we need to go through in order to heal and release all forms of abuse issues. Acceptance is one of these. So many people think that the best way of dealing with childhood abuse is to bury it, put it in the past and get on with life and living. This would be grand if it actually worked but we carry the emotional baggage and the patterns and imprints forward with us. Most people who have been abused would be shocked to realise the extent to which these issues are still playing out on a daily basis and many would not connect these things with the original abuse.

We have seen what a large part denial plays where there has been abuse. We need to be willing to stop denying the things that have happened and the effects they have had on us. We also need to let the feelings and awareness come to the surface so that they may be cleared and processed and are not allowed to cause any further damage in our lives.

Acceptance is essential if we are going to move on from the abuse. Without acceptance we stay stuck in it. What we resist will persist. When we are in a state of denial or resistance the issues will often get bigger and bigger in order to grab our attention and be dealt with. There are many things that can be included in the acceptance. First, we need to accept that the abuse took place. It is amazing how often we can fudge round this issue and try not to call it what it is. We also have to accept who did this to us and not make excuses for them or try to protect their identity. This only need be acknowledged to ourselves, this is a private process. We may also need to accept that the people who should have protected us from the abuse failed to do so. Once again the temptation may be to try and protect or excuse these people. This is not helpful at this stage, that understanding can be brought in later. We also need to accept ALL the emotions that have been created out of the abuse and not try to stuff them down. Finally, we need to accept the damage to our lives that has been caused by the abuse. This may be quite challenging as we often do not want to admit the full extent of this. We may become quite adept at hiding this damage from the world behind our carefully cultivated facades. This whole process requires us to be very honest with ourselves. There may also be some positives that we can accept. This may be the drive to succeed or a determination to help others who have been abused or marginalised or an increased understanding and compassion for the human race.

Once we have a complete sense of acceptance for what is, we can then move through this to create what we want to be, do, feel and think. Acceptance is always in a state of flow, it changes as we do and adapts to the new circumstance that we find ourselves in.

Within acceptance we can find inner peace and happiness no matter what circumstances we find ourselves in. We are not dependent on other people and outside situations to make us happy, this is within our own power.

FINDING THE AUTHENTIC SELF

Where there has been any form of abuse we will often define ourselves by what has happened to us rather than who we are.

Each and every one of us has a true authentic self that is totally wonderful. Most of us have lost touch with this amazing individual that we really are. It is buried beneath a mass of illusions that we have bought into and created as our reality. One of the most powerful things we can do is to resurrect our authentic selves and banish all the damage that we believe to be who we are. Abuse will serve to increase the damage and illusions and take us further away from who we truly are.

Not only are our authentic selves buried under the damage from childhood but they are also hidden behind the elaborate facade that we erect in order to disguise our damage. This facade will usually begin to form in adolescence when we are coming into our adult selves. The facades that we construct are usually the exact opposite of how we perceive our damage to be. If we feel that we are bad, wicked or angry we might create a facade of being very nice and caring. If we feel that we are unworthy or not good enough, we will try to prove that we are by achieving and being a success. If we feel small, vulnerable and defenceless, we may create a facade that is strong, tough and aggressive. An abuser will often create a charming, thoughtful exterior. (so beware!) If we feel chaotic and out of control, we may adopt a very controlling facade. The fact is that the stronger the facade, the more damage we are trying to hide behind it.

We are all very good at assessing a person based on what they want us to believe about them rather than what is true. This happens time and again in relationships, in job interviews and in friendships and it is only later when the damage begins to emerge from behind the facade that we get a bit of a shock. I try to encourage people not to be fooled by the wrapping but to work out what it is trying to disguise.

In reality we are neither our damage nor our facade but the real authentic self will only emerge if we are prepared to do the work to heal and release the damage. Virtually all the negativity that is in the world is created out of illusion and damage and we can see how destructive it is. There are many people who will remain stuck in their damage and never move on. We need to recognise that we cannot rescue these people and no matter how much love we heap on them we cannot dissolve away the hurt and anger that have been created. We can only rescue our own authentic selves. There are a great many people who are too damaged to sustain a good relationship or friendship and we may need to give them a wide berth.

We will not dismantle our facades until we have healed and released a significant amount of our damage, so this has to be our priority. We will probably find that we begin to unconsciously relax our facades when this takes place.

The ultimate goal that we can aspire to is to bring our true authentic selves to the forefront and align them with outer adult selves and inner child selves. Very few people ever achieve this but we can use it as an ideal to aim for.

FORGIVENESS

Virtually every religion and philosophy will preach forgiveness. Where there has been abuse, there will be a great deal to forgive and it may involve more than just the abusers themselves.

When we forgive someone it is not anything that we give to them it is a huge gift that we give to ourselves. We cannot be totally free if we do not forgive those who have trespassed against us. Forgiveness is the ultimate letting go and it represents the final chapter in the healing process. Mostly the people we are forgiving will not even be aware that we have done so.

There is often huge resistance to forgiving someone who has hurt or seemingly destroyed us. Often we believe that the only way that we have of punishing our abusers is with our anger and hate. It may feel as if we are letting them off the hook by forgiving them and that the forgiveness is somehow saying that what they did was all right. I will stress again that the reality is that forgiveness will let us off the hook that keeps us locked in the abuse issues. Our anger and hatred only punish ourselves and not the abusers. They are not party to what is going on in our minds and bodies and they would probably not care anyway.

The reason why forgiveness comes at the end of the healing process is that there is a great deal of work to be done before forgiveness can take place. We cannot forgive on top of anger. Even if the anger is suppressed within us, the forgiveness is not going to take hold. The anger is a very powerful emotion and it pervades into every aspect of our lives. The process of releasing anger will be an ongoing one and the litmus test of whether it is sufficiently dealt with will be our ability to forgive our abusers.

Forgiveness is not simply a matter of saying the words "I forgive you." Words are totally meaningless. We pay lip service to the concept of forgiveness all the time. Forgiveness is actually a state of being, a feeling and there is no mistaking it when we feel it. It is like being set free and unshackled from something that has kept us in bondage for a long time. It is cutting the final tie that binds us to the abuse and the abuser.

No one needs to know that we have forgiven if we do not want them to, least of all the abuser. It is a very personal process. Many people find that once this has occurred they are able to see the person in a totally different light. They may be able to see them as vulnerable victims rather than the cruel abuser and this changes the whole dynamic. We often build them up in our minds fed by our fear and anger and we lose touch with the fact that these people are powerless, hurt and in many ways totally pathetic.

Often we feel we can only give forgiveness if the person involved has said sorry to us first. There is often a huge need to hear our abusers apologise for what they have done. This is not a realistic expectation. The forgiveness needs to be unconditional. Even if we are still in contact with the abuser, it is unlikely that they would admit to the abuse let alone apologise for it.

The forgiveness process has to also extend to ourselves. This is possibly even more important than forgiving our abusers. We need to forgive ourselves for any hurt or abuse that we have passed on to the family and others. We also need to forgive ourselves for what we have done to abuse ourselves or to not nurture or support ourselves sufficiently. This again may be far harder to do if we are locked into the belief that we are bad or unworthy so the clearing work for these beliefs needs to be completed before our self-forgiveness can take place.

PROTECTING CHILDREN

We have seen how patterns of abuse pass down through the generations but there are some patterns born out of abuse that can go to the other extreme and create a different set of problems for the children in the long run.

There is a very strong tendency in parents to compensate their children for the things that they themselves did not receive. For instance, if the parent was shy and lacking in confidence as a child, he or she might constantly be boosting their child, praising and telling it that it is the best, etc. If the child was not unconfident in the first place this may make them arrogant or an egomaniac. If a parent came from a poor or deprived background, it may compensate for this by heaping toys or material things on the child who becomes spoilt and unaware of the value of things. This pattern is another form of projection. Here instead of projecting anger, pain or negative beliefs onto the child, the parent thinks it is doing something very positive so that the child will not suffer as it did. The intention may be good but the consequences will not be.

How this pattern plays out in abuse cases is that the parents will try to protect the child in the way that their parents failed to do. They may see danger or potential for harm all the time. They may wrap them up in cotton wool and not let them out alone. They may prevent them from going anywhere or doing anything without the parent present. They might project their fear onto the child making it feel scared without knowing what the danger is. This can have very negative consequences and create a great deal of resentment. Fear is very corrosive, it can rule us and limit who we are and what we do.

In an ideal world a child needs space in which to learn, grow and make its mistakes. A parent's role is to create loving, firm, safe and nurturing boundaries around that space to provide security. As a child gets older the boundaries get wider until it is ready to break free into the world on its own. When these boundaries are kept too tight, they will stunt a child's growth and it will probably be unable to launch into the big world as a strong independent human being. This creates a great deal of harm.

There is a very fine balance between over and under protectiveness and this is going to be harder to achieve where there has been abuse. The first unbreakable rule needs to be **NEVER, EVER** leave your child with the person or people who have abused you **EVEN** if other people are present at the time. If you have to be in contact with that person make sure you are present and watching the children every moment.

Also be aware that if sexual abuse is in the family, other members of the clan may also have been abused and be a possible abuser, so do not automatically assume that your children will be safe with them. Put in the safeguards without alerting the family or alarming the children. You can never be too careful in these instances, so err on the side of caution.

To protect children from abuse in the wider community, it is essential to give children the tools they need to deal with any situation in advance. Again there needs to be a balance here. Try not to scare the child or go into too much detail but have a drill prepared. Tell the child from a very early age that its body is a wonderful thing but no one is allowed to touch it inappropriately. Give the child the ultimate tool of saying NO to anything that does not feel right. Get them to practice saying this. Let the child know that if anyone says or does something that it is not comfortable with, the child should tell. They will be believed and never blamed for what has happened. This is important as the fear of being blamed or getting into trouble will usually ensure the child's silence.

Create an open relationship with the children where they feel free to discuss or talk about any subject. This often requires the parent to have no outward reaction to their admissions. If a child thinks that its parent will be afraid, angry or hurt, it will withold information to protect the parent. Any reaction can come later. Watch for any changes in the child's behaviour. Note where it has been and what it has done that might have caused them. Investigate if need be. Don't be afraid to ask questions even of the person who may be suspect. If a child is not happy going to someone's house or doing some activity, NEVER insist upon it.

In the arena of sexual abuse, knowledge and awareness is power. Listen to your intuition and do not override it. It will always tell us who may or may not be trusted. Most of us brush these thoughts aside or do not dare to act on them.

As a child gets older, if you have been abused, you could let it know. This will help it to understand you and also raise its awareness of what can happen in the world.

PART II

HEALING

AND RELEASING

ABUSE ISSUES

HEALING AND RELEASING

ABUSE ISSUES

In part I of this book I have shown the patterns, feelings and beliefs that are created with all forms of abuse. In my opinion, knowing and understanding the issues is not enough to remove them from your life. In part two I am giving the opportunity to clear and release the damage that is the residue of abuse.

Many of the processes given in this section are methods that I have developed and used with my clients. Some may need to be repeated particularly if you are not quite ready to deal with the issues or if there is resistance.

Intention is one of the most powerful forces that we can work with. When we put an intention behind anything that we do, we magnify the effectiveness of any of the work done. Put out the intention of releasing yourself from the bondage of abuse while doing these processes.

In my philosophy it is essential to get to the source of the issue and to do the healing at the point where the abuse took place, in this instance in childhood. Most people try to compensate for the damage created in the child within in the adult self. This can create as many problems as it tries to solve. We may take on a strong powerful, impenetrable, adult persona. We may be successful and take no negativity from anyone. In all outward appearances there may be no signs of any damage. The healing has to take place within the child aspect. This is where the powerlessness, the anger and the low self-esteem are lurking. They may only emerge in the adult at various times but we all know how we feel inside, no matter how good our facade may be.

I will also stress here that most of the damage of abuse is sitting in the **UNCONSCIOUS** mind. Most of this will be dormant for a great deal of the time and you are probably functioning pretty well in most areas of your life. It is often in times of stress or when trigger factors come into play that the issues are resurrected. Just know that to be unconscious of the damage is not the same as having released it. Most of the processes will involve working with the unconscious. Do not be fooled by what the conscious mind may think.

It would be preferable to do the clearing in this part of the book in the order it is presented. If any particular aspect is proving to be a stumbling block, leave it and come back to it at a later date. Note that this will usually be something that is pertinent to you and will require extra attention.

GOOD LUCK

RESISTANCE

Many people who read this book will not get past reading about the issues even if the damage of abuse is badly affecting their lives. There is often a huge resistance to doing the things that would help and nurture us. This resistance is provided by the ego mind. It will say things like:

You are all right the way you are

You don't have time now, do it later.

It is all a load of rubbish and doesn't work anyway.

Don't put yourself through it.

Don't open a can of worms that you cannot contain.

You don't deserve to be free of this.

You are not good enough to do this

and many more.

Expect this to happen and try not to believe the propaganda the ego puts out to sabotage you. Often falling at the first hurdle of resistance will serve to reinforce the guilt, shame and negative beliefs about yourself. Abuse is an issue that plays into the hands of resistance.

Where there is resistance you will find a million and one things to do rather than the healing and clearing work needed.

TIPS FOR RELEASING RESISTANCE

1) Be aware when resistant thoughts or feelings emerge and know that this is the ego trying to sabotage you. Do not give your power away to the ego by believing the false propaganda it is presenting.

2) There is often huge fear of change or of the unknown and consequently you may think it is safer to stay in what is familiar and therefore comfortable. **KNOW** this fear to be an illusion. Counteract the fear by repeating the following statement. **I AM OPEN TO CHANGE AND CREATING A NEW POSITIVE REALITY FOR MYSELF.** Keep saying this until all residue of fear is dissolved.

3) When the resistance surfaces, do not go into conflict or battle with it. Be an objective observer of it and know that resistance is often a sign that we are wanting to make changes for the better.

4) **SURRENDER.** This is your best possible weapon against resistance. Put your trust in the process. Keep repeating to yourself **I SURRENDER TO THE PROCESS.** Surrender does not mean you lose, it simply means that you are not willing to fight the battle.

5) Trust that it will all be easy and effortless and that each bit will be done in its right space and time. This is programming the unconscious to flow with the process.

6) **GET SUPPORT.** Ask for help from friends or a partner. It may help doing the processes with someone who has been through similar issues.

7) If it is within your belief system, ask for help from a higher power and surrender the reins of control to your higher self. Know that it would not want anything for you that is not for your highest good.

8) Be kind to yourself and schedule time and space for yourself to do your clearing work. Take the phone off the hook and put your own needs before others for a change.

REMOVING THE PROGRAM OF ABUSE

The cycle and pattern of abuse will vary for each individual but it will follow similar lines. The unconscious mind works a lot like a computer. Whatever is programmed into it will be what manifests in your life. The program and cycle will play out without any conscious interference on your part.

It is necessary to become conscious of the various points within this pattern. This involves the reactions, the feelings and the beliefs. Note whether there is a compulsion to self-abuse or to take the feelings out on someone else or both.

1) Raise your awareness of your particular abuse program.

2) What is the trigger that sets the whole cycle in motion? Does someone say or do something that brings up feelings of powerlessness or anger or hurt? How do you react to this? Do you project the feelings outward or inward? If inward, what does it compel you to do? e.g. Eat, drink, beat yourself up, become depressed. If you put the energy outward who is the person or

people that you take these feelings out on? e.g. spouse, children, co-workers, friends. How do you feel when you have done this to yourself or others? What beliefs do you have about yourself as a result? e.g. I am a bad person, I deserve to be treated badly, I am unworthy, life is awful. Write all the various aspects of the pattern down, including as many of the emotions and beliefs that you are aware of.

3) Have the intention of removing this program and pattern and all the various feelings and beliefs associated.

Take some time when you will not be disturbed. Take the phone off the hook. Sit comfortably and start to take some deep breaths to relax the body and still the mind..... Put your focus onto the solar plexus..... You are working with the inner self and unconscious mind. Take your attention back to the initial time of the abuse as far back as you can remember..... From this time a program has been created that you are now commanding the unconscious mind to delete and erase from its memory banks..... You are deleting any sense of powerlessness and helplessness, any fear, any anger, guilt, hurt or shame..... You are erasing any belief that you are bad, wicked, being punished or deserve to have this thing happen..... You are also deleting any self-destructive patterns that have occurred as a result of this abuse or any desire to render other people powerless by using control or abuse on them..... Command that all these elements be removed from the programming of the unconscious self..... See them going into a floppy disc or video tape..... Press the eject button and see it emerging from the unconscious and computer mind..... Throw the disc or tape into a bonfire and see it shrivel up never to be used again.

You now want to put in a new program..... Ask the unconscious mind to bring in a new understanding and pattern..... See the young child at the same age..... Bring in an awareness that the issue is with the abuser and not with the child. The child has the power of choice and can walk away or say NO to anything it doesn't want..... Nothing that goes on around it is personal to the child, it is circumstantial.... The child is strong, safe and secure and it feels compassion and pity for the damage this person has sustained but it knows that it is not part of that..... See the child refusing to take the baton of abuse and walking away from the situation unscathed..... See this new program being put into the unconscious computer mind. Command the unconscious to bring in this new awareness into your daily life. When you are ready bring your focus back into the room.

This process focuses on releasing the unconscious programming. This will also need to be done on a more conscious level. It can only be done as and when the issue and cycle is triggered. Know in advance how you usually react and feel when this occurs. CHOOSE to do it differently. At first it does not matter what you do as long as it breaks the pattern. Gradually look at what you would like to feel, think and do and bring this in. For instance, your husband or boss shouts at you for no reason, you might normally feel hurt and angry, withdraw from them or go into a sulk and then reach for the biscuit tin or a drink, feeling unloved or unappreciated. In the new pattern you could recognise that they are the ones with the problem and either remove yourself from them or let them know that it is not acceptable to be treated in this way. Go for a walk or ring a friend but do something that supports you and not abuses you. This needs to be preplanned or you will go into your old pattern without thinking.

TAKING POWER BACK FROM YOUR ABUSERS

This process needs to be done for all types of abuse.

I would remind you that power is the central issue within all forms of abuse. The abuser is essentially coming from a position of powerlessness due to abuse or neglect in childhood. They try to feel better by making someone else feel powerless and making themselves feel powerful. This is external power and the effects are very short lived since it does not actually remove the inner feelings of powerlessness. This then sets up the power addiction that continues the cycle of abuse.

Trying to get power or control as an adult does not actually change anything for the child inside. This is why it is essential to do this process at the age you were when the abuse first took place. It is the child who gave the power away and it needs to take it back. This is internal and not external power.

Although I have looked at the different forms of abuse separately in this book, it is not uncommon to be the victim of all three and sometimes at the hands of the same person.

1) Make a list of the people who have abused you. If you do not know who the person was give them some identifying feature.

2) Put the ages you were when the abuse with each person started.

3) It may help to find pictures of yourself at these various ages.

4) Within the inner and unconscious self all time is one and all ages you have been will be contained inside.

VISUALISATION

Take some time and space for yourself. You are going to take your power back from those who you have given it away to through abuse. If you have more than one person to deal with, start with the most recent one. Sit comfortably and start to take some deep breaths into the solar plexus to relax the body and still the mind..... Within your inner self and unconscious mind you are going back in time to the age you were when you first gave your power away to your abuser..... See the child at this age..... See yourself as you are now going to that child. Let it know that you are there to guide and support it and help it through the obstacles of life...... Give it a big hug and explain that you are going to help it to take its power back from its abusers..... Stand behind the child with your hands on its shoulders..... Call in the abuser and see him or her standing a few feet in front of you, facing you..... You are now commanding the inner self to recall and revoke any power you have given away to this person..... It is as if there is a big magnet in your solar plexus pulling back tiny globules of golden energy and power from this person.... See these going into your solar plexus and joining together like golden mercury..... As your power comes back to you, you notice that the power the this person has is what you gave him..... See him as weak pathetic and afraid without your energy to live on..... Tell the child that it has the power to say NO to this person..... Tell the child to say this outloud..... Keep doing this until the word is said with power and conviction..... When there is no more power coming back and the child can stand in its power and say NO knowing that no one will override this directive, turn away from the abuser and walk away with the child..... Tell it how proud of it you are and let it know that no one may do anything to it that it does not choose or want..... Place the empowered child in your heart and come back forward in time..... Bring your attention back into the room.....

Repeat this process with any other people you have given your power to.

DEALING WITH EMOTIONAL SHUTDOWN

I have described in part I how many people shutdown their emotions after any form of abuse. This is a protective mechanism that removes the victim from the pain, anger and guilt created by abuse. While this might seem to help in the short term it will have very destructive consequences in the long run. However, it may not just be our emotions that we disconnect from as a result of abuse. There may be a great deal of disgust with the physical body and many people disconnect from it. Quite naturally there may be a cut off from sexual energy. When there has been a trauma or difficult situation, we often separate from our spirit, which is our most important source of love and nurture. In order to be whole again, it is necessary to reintegrate all these parts of yourself as they have a vital role to play in your life. You will find it very difficult to release or be free of negative emotions if you are in a state of shutdown.

1) Check out what parts of yourself you have disconnected from. e.g. Your emotions, your body, your sexuality, your spirit.

2) Be willing to reconnect with these areas.

3) Listen to the fears your ego will present in response to choosing to reconnect. Do not give them power by believing them.

4) There may be a semi or part time disconnection with your various aspects.

5) Put out the intention of making the connection with all parts of yourself, acknowledging that your life can improve immeasurably as a result.

Take some time and space when you will not be disturbed. Sit comfortably and take some deep breaths to relax the body and still the mind...... Become aware of your spine. This is the superhighway that links all parts of the body. As a result of abuse and other traumas and difficulties you may have become unplugged..... See these as electric cables with plugs at the end. The disconnections will be at the neck area of the spine..... The first part to reconnect with is the physical body...... See a red cable coming right up from the base of the spine. Put the plug into its corresponding socket of the red cable. Sense a gentle pulse of energy going right down the spine and extending to the legs and feet..... Take a moment to focus your attention on any physical sensations in the body. Welcome it..... Ask the physical body to convey to you what its needs and dislikes are so that you may provide for them. Have a sense of love for the physical body JUST AS IT IS.....

Next you are going to connect with your sexual energy. This is an orange cord and socket and its source is a few inches above the base of the spine. Reconnect this cord at the neck and feel the powerful kundalini energy coming up the spine and flowing gently..... Breathe deeply and set the loop in action.

The emotions are the next reconnection. Here the cord is yellow and the source is the spine opposite the solar plexus...... Remember once the emotions are able to flow, you can evict the hurt and anger and feel the positive feelings...... Command the unconscious mind to reconnect the emotions disregarding any previous commands to the contrary..... See the yellow plug connecting into the socket and feel the change in energy..... Take a deep breath into the solar plexus to make the connections with the emotions.

The next point you want to touch on is the heart..... The cord is pink and connects with self love. It is at heart level on the spine. See the plug and socket reuniting and feel a warmth spreading through your body.

The final connection is with the spirit. The purple or white cord is coming from the top of the head and the socket is once again in the neck of the spine..... See the plug connecting with the socket and anchor the spirit into the body..... Command the unconscious mind to heal any sense of separation from the higher self..... Feel this wonderful energy flowing into every single cell of the body.

If at anytime in the future you disconnect from any of these aspects, simply see the plug connecting with the socket once again. When you are ready bring your full attention back into the room.

HEALING AND RELEASING EMOTIONS OF ABUSE

Releasing the emotions of abuse has got to be the single most important thing to do if you want to be free of the destruction of abuse. We have seen in part one that both the avoidance of these emotions and the way in which they manifest in your life will create most of the long term problems from abuse.

Many people will be in denial that they have these emotions because they have effectively buried them or manage to mask them with work or substances. Do not be fooled into believing that you have no emotional response to your abuse or that you must have dealt with the feelings because you are no longer in touch with them.

Most of our emotions spend the majority of the time in the suppressed position. In order to be free of them we have to allow them to surface, to be with them and then expel them outward and away. This is a private process, no one else need be involved, least of all the people the emotions are about.

All of our emotions will not disappear overnight. There are many levels and layers that are involved and these will only present themselves over time. This is a good thing, it means that we will not be overwhelmed and will therefore be able to deal with each layer as it emerges. Fear will tell us that if we get in touch with our emotions it will be like a dam bursting so it is better to leave well alone and carry on as before. This is not true.

There are many different ways that we can work with the emotions and I will cover as many as possible.

DEALING WITH EMOTIONS WHEN THEY SURFACE

1) Have a willingness to be honest with yourself and not to go into denial about your feelings.

2) Bring in the powerful force of intention to aid you in this process. The intention to be free of your negative emotions.

3) Become aware of yourself and what is going on inside and around you.

4) Become conscious of the unconscious patterns you employ to avoid, distract or mask your negative feelings. This may be food, cigarettes, alcohol, etc. or it may be keeping busy, work, television, computers or sport. Often we are doing this activity or reaching for this thing as the emotion begins to emerge and we never give the feeling a chance to surface. This will be an automatic reaction, no conscious thought is involved.

5) When the compulsion to put in an avoidance action takes place **STOP**. Remove yourself from other people and just **BE** with what is going on. Let the emotions surface.

6) Identify what the emotion or emotions are. Are you feeling angry, frustrated, hurt, afraid or guilty. They may not be too easily defined. **YOU KNOW WHEN A NEGATIVE EMOTION HAS SURFACED BECAUSE YOU DO NOT FEEL GOOD.**

7) Note what occurred to bring these emotions up. Did something happen or someone say or do something. The triggers are often very subtle and unconscious.

8) You do not need to remain in the emotion for many minutes. Focus on the feelings and the sensations in the physical body but do not try to control them.

9) Speed up the releasing of the emotion by expelling it on the breath with force. You should be able to hear the breath leaving the body. Keep doing this until the feeling subsides.

10) Do something nice for yourself. Have a bath or go for a walk or buy yourself some flowers.

This process works for the emotions that surface but does not actually address the underlying emotions created by the abuse. In my philosophy it is only when we get to the source of an issue or emotion that it can be released. I liken it to a fountain or a leak. We can get buckets and deal with the water that appears or we can go to the source and mend it. This way we do not have to be constantly bailing out the feelings created.

Emotions come from the child aspect of ourselves and consequently it is the child that initially felt them. Anger expressed through the adult does not seem to reduce the anger inside because the child is still full of anger.

The following process can be used to work with all the emotions of abuse at once or individually. Do not overload yourself or rush the process. You may need to do it more than once.

I see this process as clearing out an inner junk room where we store all our unexpressed emotions. This junk room is located in the solar plexus, our emotional centre. Just like a junk room all the stuff is packed in boxes, bin bags and old suitcases and these are the symbolic things that we want to remove. We also use a bonfire to burn up all this emotional junk. In this process both the adult and child aspects come into play. The adult supports the child and instructs it in what to do.

1) The child inside that we need to access is at the age when the abuse finished or if it were a single incident like rape, at that time. If you have a photograph of yourself at this age, refresh your memory as to how you looked and felt at the time. Often our emotions shine out or we may look defensive.

2) Put willingness and intention into allowing the child inside to feel, if only momentarily, the emotions so that they may be released.

3) Let go any resistance to this process by SURRENDER-ING and handing over control to your higher self.

Take some time when you won't be disturbed. Sit comfortably and take some deep breaths allowing the breath to go as low as possible in the body..... With every out breath feel yourself letting go and relaxing..... Keep doing this until you feel a connection with your inner self..... Your focus of attention is on the solar plexus, your emotional centre..... Ask your unconscious mind to take you back in time to the age you were when the abuse ended..... Have a sense of this child or adolescent. Look and feel how it is feeling, are your emotions showing or hidden behind a mask? See you as you are now and go to that child and put an arm around it..... Explain to it that you love it and are here to help it release the residue of emotion from its abuse..... Let it know that it was not responsible or deserving of that abuse and that to hold onto any emotions from the abuse will result in its being punished for something it has not done and the abuser wins.... Let it know that it is safe to release the emotional baggage so that it does not have to carry it round..... Support the child through the letting go process..... The first emotions to be dealt with are guilt and shame. Tell the child that the only person who should feel any guilt and shame is the abuser. Guilt is a choice and you can make the decision not to feel it..... Command the unconscious mind to remove and delete any belief that you are guilty..... Allow the feelings of guilt to be released and expelled from the body. Use the breath to forcefully remove the physical feelings of guilt from the body. See the emotional junk room and all the baggage marked guilt and see the child putting each one into the bonfire. Still breathing the emotions through..... When all the baggage of guilt is removed, give the child a big hug and let it know that no matter what has happened in the past, it is still pure and innocent..... It need never perceive itself as guilty nor invite the punishment that accompanies a belief in guilt.

The next emotion to remove from the body is shame. Be with the child and tap into the aspects of the abuse that have created this sense of shame..... You only need to feel this emotion for a few moments. Recreate any image you may need to connect with the emotion..... Command the unconscious mind and inner self to release this feeling and expel it with the breath forcefully..... See the boxes of shame going into the bonfire.... Note where in your body the physical sensation of shame is..... Put an imaginary trough or pipe into that area with the other end going into the bonfire and see this thick black tar like substance coming away from that area..... keep the trough in place until no more substance comes out..... Visualise light going into the area cleansing and clearing any last residue..... Let the child know that it has no cause to feel any shame as it has done nothing wrong.....

Anger and hatred are the next emotions to deal with. These may be buried quite deep. Reassure the child that it is quite safe to release the anger in this process. No one will be hurt and there will be no backlash or comeback onto it. Bring the memory of the abuser to the forefront of your mind. If it was a stranger, have a representation of them. See the enormity of what they have done to the child and allow the natural anger from the abuse to the surface. Do not try to protect, defend or excuse the abuser at this stage. Let the child be angry at this thing done to it that it didn't want. In the child's imagination see the person in front of it and encourage it to express the its anger in whatever way it wants. It can shout out or punch or hit the representation of the abuser. (No one will be hurt in reality.) Breathe the anger out of the body **VERY** forcefully. Hurl the boxes and baggage of anger and hate out of the junk room and into the bonfire. Encourage the child to keep expressing and expelling the feeling until there is nothing left. In order for this to work optimally, the actual feeling of anger needs to be felt but only momentarily. Praise the child for letting the emotion out. You can do the anger release for each person who has abused you. The child may also need to express its anger for the person or people who did not protect or safeguard it.

Hurt and sadness will often emerge once anger has been tapped into, they are very closely related. Let the child know that it is safe to feel and express its pain. Allow this feeling to bubble up and breathe into it and expel it from the body. Encourage the child to feel the emotional hurt. See the boxes marked pain, hurt and sadness in the junk room and put them into the flames. Breathing out all the while.

Fear is the final emotion to release. Let the child know that all the fears that have been created by the abuse are illusions and they can now be removed. Each fear has been put into a box in the junk room and is labelled. When you open any of the boxes, you find that they are empty. Throw each box into the flames, breathing away the illusions. First, fear of being hurt, fear of power, fear of authority and control, fear of shame and humiliation, fear of not being good enough, fear that you are wicked and bad, fear of betrayal, fear of insecurity etc. Breathe out the fear illusions as each of these boxes goes into the flames. The adult you can now reassure the child that it is safe, that you are looking after it and protecting it and that you will give it the tools it needs to deal with any situation that life sends its way. Tell the child how proud of it you are and that it deserves only the best things from life. Give it a big hug. When you are ready bring your attention back into the room.

People who have been abused are often very angry. This does not always show on the outside but may appear as depression, addictions or in some other way. Anger will probably need to be dealt with in a variety of ways. Be aware if you are wanting to hold onto your anger because you think you are punishing the abuser with it. This is an illusion. You are only punishing yourself. He or she will probably not even not even be aware of your angry thoughts and feelings. You are having to live with them on a daily basis.

Here are some methods for relieving you of your anger. Keep in mind that the main goal in anger release is to disperse it safely without putting it onto yourself or anyone else.

1) The simplest way to release anger is to breathe it out as soon as you are aware that you are feeling it. This needs to be done with some force as it is a very powerful emotion. Don't delay too long after the feeling has been triggered or it may go back down again.

2) The most important thing we can do to release an emotion is to express it. It is rarely advisable to do this to the people involved as they may dump their anger right back onto you and you are back to square one. I suggest doing anger burn letters. Here you write to the person putting whatever you need to say to express your feelings to him or her. This can be done

in as graphic language as you choose to use, no one is going to read this. Make sure you burn the letter as soon as it is written. This is the letting go process. Do this outside in a metal bucket if you have one. It would also be a good idea to write a letter as the child at the age it was when the abuse took place. If you were young, use your non dominant hand to do this. Use the language that a child would. You might simply want to repeat the same phrase until the anger loses its charge. This process may be done many times until there is not much anger to be in touch with.

3) Release your anger in nature. As it name suggests, nature is incredibly nurturing. Go for a walk and breathe, stomp, throw sticks or stones. Put out the intention that you are letting the anger go. This method is particularly effective if the anger is sitting in depressive feelings. Breathe deeply and strongly to dislodge the emotion.

4) If you are in a big time anger mode, the best solution is probably to physicalise and vocalise it. Make sure you will not alarm people or animals. Use any sports bat or broom handle and put pillows on a bed and hit them until the anger dissipates. If you add your voice to this, it is more powerful. A one word insult repeated constantly is very effective. You could also use a punch bag but make sure you use gloves to absorb the anger.

5) The car is a wonderful place to release anger, not as road rage I must stress. It is insulated from the world and you can shout and scream with impunity.

DEALING WITH GUILT ON A DAILY BASIS

Guilt is always a choice we make. In letting your guilt go from the past, you need to make a daily decision not to let it back in again. To do this you have to believe that you do not deserve it.

1) Reinforce daily " I deserve to be free of all guilt and punishment."

2) Become aware of your patterns with guilt. Who makes you feel guilty? Is this something that comes just from you or have you given your power to people who manipulate you with guilt? How do you respond when you feel guilty? How do you punish yourself? Do you play other people's games because you feel guilty?

3) Once you know your patterns you can begin to break them. Take your power back. Choose not to play any game that others put out. Do not go into a beat yourself up mode. CHOOSE not to feel guilty.

4) Consciously do things that reward rather than punish you. Each time reinforce how much you deserve these things.

5) Keep telling the child inside that it is innocent no matter what happened in the past.

RELEASING PATTERNS OF PROTECTION

Once you have been abused the priority will often be to protect yourself from further hurt or abuse. These protective mechanisms will often come into play once the danger is past. This is a clear case of shutting the stable door after the horse has bolted. Virtually every means used to protect yourself will actually create more hurt and pain in the long run. **THEY DO NOT WORK.** It is therefore essential that these mechanisms be dismantled as part of the healing process. Many of them will have been brought in unconsciously. I will list the probable protection patterns employed.

1) Emotional shutdown. By removing yourself from your feelings you may believe yourself to be safe from the negative legacy of abuse.

2) Weight as protection. This will seem like it is giving some physical protection and will seem to make you safe by not attracting any unwanted sexual advances. The result is that you feel bad and you do not attract any wanted sexual advances.

3) Putting on a tough prickly hard shell. This keeps people at arms length and stops them getting too close. The downside is that you attract a great deal of aggression from other people, who are mirroring your energy and you end up lonely, isolated, hurt and rejected.

4) Using substances. You may use the substances to protect you from your emotions but the damage they do to your body, your relationships and your ability to function in every day life is far more destructive.

5) Working all the time or keeping busy. This removes you from any emotional contact. It breaks up relationships and families causing huge pain.

6) You use control and power. By taking control you may think you are protecting yourself from being controlled. You end up losing the love and respect that you crave, including your own.

8) A drive to succeed and be independent. This cuts out the need to allow others to meet your needs and possibly be let down and hurt by them. You may hide behind an amazing persona that people admire but few can get near.

Look at this list and note whether any of these protection mechanisms apply to you. You may find that you work with more than one. I guarantee that the means you use to protect yourself creates more pain in the long run.

You will only be able to start to dismantle your means of protection once you have begun to release the emotions that they are protecting. If you do not want to feel your pain, anger, shame and guilt, it makes no sense to lock them up inside and have to post armed protection twenty four hours a day for something you do not want in the first place. Remove the feelings and you have no need of protection.

Once the emotions and the protection are released you can allow your wonderful quality of positive vulnerability to come through. This and your intuition are the only protection you need.

1) Look at what protection mechanisms you employ. You might have some other than those listed.

2) Look specifically at what you are protecting from. Are you protecting yourself from your own feelings? Are you protecting yourself from people coming into your life and hurting you? Are you protecting yourself from your sexuality and sexual advances? Are you protecting yourself from further abuse by cutting off from people? Are you running away from yourself?

3) Look at the patterns of your personal mechanisms. You may not have consciously been aware of how these play out.

4) Notice the extent to which they are not working for you. Look at how they are simply perpetuating the negative aspects of abuse. Have a plus and minus column. If you have more pluses than minuses, you are probably not ready to release them. You will be clinging to an illusion that they DO protect you. You will probably need to release more emotions.

5) Begin to change the patterns. This can be done in small ways. For instance, if you are aware that with strangers you put up barriers and become aloof, make an effort to be open and friendly, or if when an emotion surfaces you dive for the ice cream, stop yourself and just sit with it and let it go. This will be a gradual and conscious process but it does not have to be difficult.

6) Allow yourself to let some vulnerability out. This does not have to be negative things like pain and fear. It may be innocence, intimacy or honesty or a childlike play mode. Do not be afraid of it, it is your best friend.

LETTING GO OF ADDICTIONS

I have shown in part I that addiction plays a huge part in abuse patterns and this may be one of the hardest parts to crack. As with any addiction a great deal of determination and will power is needed to get through the withdrawal phase. These will usually be a physical or chemical addiction as well as an emotional one. This applies even when there is no physical substance involved. There may be an adrenaline rush or some other physical reaction to the addiction. Common addictions associated with abuse are: -

1) Power - through control or being in positions of authority.

2) Power - through abusing others.

3) Food. Mainly junk food, chocolate, sugar or wheat products.

4) Cigarettes.

5) Alcohol.

6) Recreational drugs.

7) Prescription drugs.

8) Self- harming.

9) Work.

10) Sex.

11) Shopping.

12) Computer games or the Internet.

13) Sport or dangerous pastimes.

14) Television or videos.

Most of these things are normal aspects of life or living. However, when they become an addiction they take you over and can be extremely destructive.

1) Do you have any addictions. Be honest here. Are there any cravings that you have. If you are not sure, ask yourself how you would feel if you did not have that thing for a week or month.

2) You may have more than one addiction. If so put them in order of importance.

3) What is the pay-off to doing or having this thing. It may have reached the stage that the only pay-off is avoiding the inevitable withdrawal. Be honest and write it down.

4) What are the disadvantages? e.g. It costs money, it takes up a great deal of time, it removes you from friends and family, you beat yourself up afterwards, you feel used. Write these things down.

5) Compare the pros and cons and make a conscious decision as to whether you are ready to give up the addiction. You have to mean this or it will all come to nothing.

6) GET SUPPORT. This may be a professional organisation, friends or family. Don't expect them to do it for you.

7) Take your power back from the substance or activity. You have given it your power and so it has been controlling you. Take it back and see it for what it is and not what you have made it.

8) Set up a schedule. You will want to start reducing the thing you are addicted to over time to help with any withdrawal symptoms. Set a date for the cold turkey. Make sure this is realistic and keep reinforcing to yourself that from that date you are not going to use the substance.

9) Prepare in advance. Make sure you have none of the substance around to tempt you or plan distractions to remove you from the withdrawal. Have plenty of alternative things available to fill the void without transferring the addiction.

10) Know that you are going to have to feel some feelings in the withdrawal phase. Be prepared for this and prepare those around you. BE with your emotions when they arise and allow them to process through. Breathing out will help this.

11) Exercise your will power and give yourself treats and rewards for your achievements.

12) Some of these addictions are part of your life and will have to be reintroduced gently back into your existence once the cravings have gone. Do not allow yourself to be drawn back into your old patterns and habits.

13) Do not beat yourself up if you fail. There is still more clearing that is needed before you are ready. Start the process again at a later date.

14) Even if you do succeed, be aware that at times of stress or trauma it may be easy to slip back into the addiction. Build up safeguards to prevent this happening.

DEALING WITH WEIGHT ISSUES

There are two distinct areas when looking at weight issues within abuse. There is the weight used as protection and food used as a means of dealing with emotions. Many people will be working with both these issues.

WEIGHT FOR PROTECTION

Ask yourself:-

1) Do you use weight to protect you from sexual advances?

2) How would it feel without the weight and being a sexual being out in the world? Would you feel vulnerable or comfortable with this?

3) Do you hide behind your weight?

4) Does your weight make you feel more or less visible?

5) Do you feel safe in your world?

6) On a scale of 1-10 how ready are you to be without the weight. Note that what you may think on a conscious level will not necessarily be what your inner or unconscious self will believe. You may give yourself a 10 consciously. Ask again but the unconscious this time.

Get an idea from these questions whether you feel safe enough to give up the illusion of protection that your weight gives you.

The fact is that if you are not ready, you will sabotage any attempt you make to lose the weight. You may need to do more work with the inner child. You may have spent many years feeling unsafe and in need of protection so the body will not necessarily believe you if you tell it once that you no longer need the weight. The best way that I have found to get through to the body and unconscious mind is to make a personal tape. This is better if it is done subliminally but if you do not have the means to do this just put it straight onto the tape. Here you make a series of statements that you want to change to do with your body and weight. The process is as follows.

1) Take some time and write down the things that you would like to change.

2) For each thing make a statement. Always put it in the present tense and first person singular. (I) Some general examples would be:-

a) I thank my body for protecting me in the past. I am now able to keep myself safe so I no longer need the excess weight to protect me. I command that it now be released.

b) My body craves healthy and nurturing foods.

c) I am now able to repel any unwanted sexual advances. I do not need my body to do it for me.

d) I love myself and my body and I look after all my needs.

e) It is safe for me to be attractive and visible in the world.

f) I now put my past behind me and I create my future based on who I want to be and not what others have done to me.

g) I like and accept myself just as I am.

h) I now change my pattern of punishing myself for what has happened.

i) I stop turning my anger onto myself and release it safely.

3) When you have as many statements as you can think of, you are going to put them on tape. To do this

subliminally you need a facility that has a CD or tape linked to another tape and a microphone. Put gentle relaxing music on the CD or tape. Make sure that the sound level of the microphone is just below that of the music so that the voice and words are recorded but cannot be heard. Keep repeating the statements until the end of the tape.

4) Play the tape each night just as you are dropping off to sleep but put the sound level so low that you can hardly hear it consciously. Some people find that this helps them to sleep and need not disturb anyone else in the room.

5) Change or add to the tape as you become aware of new aspects.

6) Do not expect a dramatic overnight shift. This takes time, think how long you have been stuck in these patterns. Persist because it does change in a very gentle unconscious way.

DEALING WITH COMFORT EATING.

1) Start to become aware of your patterns with food and eating. Keep a diary for one week and identify the times, feelings and types of foods you are wanting to eat.

2) Use this data to see what your patterns are. Is there a trigger like boredom, frustration, disappointment or anger? Is there a sugar or carbohydrate high and then low that brings up feelings that you want to squash?

3) What feelings do you have when you have eaten? Guilt, shame, anger, satisfaction or disgust?

4) Put your hunger level on a scale of **1-10** when you eat something.

5) What are your particular comfort foods like chocolate, chips, crisps, biscuits, cake etc?

6) Are there any particular times of day that become danger times like late at night or mid morning.?

Armed with all the information about your particular patterns and issues you can put together a personal plan to deal with them.

If you are not committed to making changes then you may as well not bother as you are only setting yourself up for failure. Just know that you are **CHOOSING** to have the weight. The food is more important to you than you are.

Remember that this is an addiction that you are dealing with and you will need to follow the addiction process. Be prepared for the withdrawal symptoms and decide to ride them through. Welcome any emotions that come to the surface as a result of breaking the addiction and let them go.

Choose not to have danger foods in the house and always have alternatives available as substitutes. Look for activities, situations and people who will provide you with genuine comfort and satisfaction rather than the illusion of it that food gives. Create new positive patterns with food and create a healthy relationship with it.

GIVING UP THE VICTIM AND TYRANT

We have already seen that there will be a victim and/or tyrant within us to a greater or lesser extent when there has been abuse. Both these modes are extremely destructive and need to be removed from the psyche and inner patterning.

Being a victim can be an addiction in itself and may be hard to give up. It will help to be aware of the various ways in which it manifests.

1) Look at the ways in which the victim is playing out in your life.

2) Do you allow other people to abuse or bully you?

3) Do you abuse or bully yourself?

4) Do you allow life to victimise you?

5) Are you unlucky? Do bad things always seem to happen to you?

6) What are the pay-offs to being a victim?

a) You let other people make choices or decisions.

b) You do you not have to take responsibility for yourself.

c) You get attention or sympathy for what happens to you.

d) You enjoy the drama of your misfortunes.

e) You have an excuse for not succeeding in life.

f) You feed off or live off other people's energy.

g) People run round and take care of you.

7) These are all very powerful pay-offs and in order to give up the victim you need to be willing to give them up and choose to create your own reality.

8) Be aware of how these pay-offs work in your life and be honest with yourself as to whether you can give them up. Know that if you are not ready, you will either sabotage the process or not even try it.

9) Also know that eventually people will get tired of all the energy they have to spend on you and the very people you depend on may turn their backs on you.

10) If you are ready and willing to give up being the victim then you have to address the abuse that created it and take back your power from the people you have given it to.

You can acknowledge the role of the tyrant in your life.

1) Do you play the bully or tyrant to anyone in your life? Who is the person or people that you do this to? Be honest. It may happen in small subtle ways. How does it feel when you do this?

2) Do you tyrannise yourself by bullying, name calling or beating yourself up for every little thing?

3) Are people aware of how nasty you are to yourself or do you hide it from them?

4) How does it feel when you tyrannise yourself?

5) Do you think you deserve this treatment?

6) Do you get any feelings of power being the tyrant even if only to yourself?

7) Is there any masochistic pleasure derived from tyrannising yourself?

8) Is this a deeply ingrained pattern or addiction?

9) Are you aware of the extent to which you have taken over the role of abuser and are probably doing a better job of it than anyone else in your life?

10) Are you willing to give up the tyranny to yourself and others?

11) What are the pay-offs?

12) What is your victim tyrant ratio? Put both numbers out of ten. For instance, if you are stuck in victim mode you may be a 9/10 but you may also choose to tyrannise yourself and be a 9/10. You will want to get both these numbers under 2/10.

If there is a willingness to give up both victim and tyrant modes, it will involve using the third option.

1) The third option requires using the power of conscious choice instead of repeating old patterns.

2) The third option means that you **CHOOSE** to be neither victim nor tyrant. Instead you use the experience of your abuse to know that this is not something that should happen to anyone let alone that you be the one who perpetrates it further by turning it onto yourself or onto another person.

3) The third option is committed to turning what was negative into a positive. This means releasing the negative aspects or choosing to perceive them differently.

4) The third option involves finding inner peace, harmony and happiness instead of living out the illusions created by abuse. This is the goal.

5) Are you willing to take the third option instead of staying stuck in the cycle of victim and tyrant?

6) If the answer is yes then know that this involves taking your power back, releasing the emotions and seeing everything that happened to you in a totally different light. What you believe you will create as your reality.

If you want a different reality, you have to change what you believe.

7) **CHOOSE** the third option **NOW**.

RAISING SELF-ESTEEM

Your self-esteem is your barometer that determines how other people and life will treat you. This is determined by the beliefs you have about yourself and how you **FEEL** about yourself. Whatever elements you have will be reflected back to you constantly.

Sadly, your self-esteem is not initially created by you but the people and circumstances that you encountered in childhood. Your self-esteem is often projected onto you based on the self-esteem of the people who are around you. **ALL THE THINGS PROJECTED ONTO YOU ARE AN ILLUSION.**

This process will require a great deal of honesty and introspection. You will have an inner self-esteem that will have been created by the child aspect and its feelings about itself. You will also have an outer self-esteem where you have tried to compensate for how you feel inside by being successful or marrying well or being the life and soul of the party. Keep these separate. If you have been abused there will probably be a huge discrepancy between them.

1) On a scale of 1-100 how high is your outer self-esteem?

2) On a scale of 1-100 how high is your inner self-esteem?

Ideally, both of these should be between 90-100. The reality will be that most people's inner self-esteem will be quite low. If the inner self-esteem is raised the outer one will go up automatically. This does not happen in reverse however. Consequently, I will be focussing on the inner self-esteem.

1) **What negative beliefs do you have about yourself?**
   Remember, this is the inner child that we are talking about.

e.g. I am not good enough.

I don't deserve love attention and good things.

I am stupid.

I am ugly.

I am boring.

People don't like me.

I am to blame when things go wrong.

I am bad or wicked.

I make people angry.

I deserve to be beaten, shouted at or abused.

I have no power.

My feelings are unacceptable.

I have to sacrifice myself for others.

I can't do anything right.

2) Beside each belief put down who made you feel this way
   or told you these things. It may be more than one
   person. Put the age you were when you were given
   each one.

3) Begin to see how each one of these things were
   projected onto you by these people and are simply a
   reflection of how they felt about themselves. **NONE** of
   these are true.

4) You can remove these beliefs from your unconscious
   programming.

5) This may be an ongoing process. As you remember
   other negative beliefs that you have been given. Not
   all of these things will have been told to you. Some

you will have deduced based on how people treated you.

6) Start with the most recent beliefs. You are going to be working with the adult and the child together as we want both of them to be in harmony. See the child at the age it was when the belief was projected. It may help to visualise you and the child working at a computer screen, removing the programs that you do not want to keep.

7) For each belief have a positive statement to hand to program in its place.

8) With each belief or projection say; " I command the unconscious mind to remove, delete and erase the belief that..... from my mind and memory banks. It was not true then and it is not true now." See the child at the age it was when the belief was created, press the delete key on the computer and see the belief being blanked from the screen. Replace it with the new positive statement. " I now program the new belief that I....." See this coming up on the screen in front of you and press enter.

9) Take the child and a give it a big mirror to hold up in front of it. See the person or people who projected this belief onto you and hold the mirror to them. Allow yourself to feel some compassion that they have these beliefs and feelings but CHOOSE not to take them on.

10) Do this for each belief as near as possible to the age you were even if this was as a baby.

11) See a barometer measuring your inner self-esteem and see the gauge going higher as you clear your emotions and beliefs.

DON'T TAKE IT PERSONALLY

Within the process of healing and release of abuse, the first phase is about letting go. You need to let go the negative emotions, the destructive beliefs and the abusive patterns of behaviour. This is an ongoing process and it can be done every time any of these things surface or come to your attention.

The next phase of the process involves changing the perceptions that we may have taken on and understanding that the abuse was never about the child, it was about the perpetrator. Everything that you have taken on board about the abuse was either projected onto you by the abuser or it was an assessment of yourself that you have created based on their actions. Neither of these will be true.

When you are a child you see everything as if you were the centre of the universe. In healing abuse you have to see the bigger picture and that you were just a pawn in a far larger game.

When you are able to do this, you can begin to see that whatever the type of abuse or whoever did this abuse it was **NEVER** personal to you. It was circumstantial. Learning not to take things personally is one of the most liberating things you can do. You will have probably spent a great deal of time trying to work out what was wrong with you or what you did wrong to deserve this abuse. The answer is **NOTHING**. Abuse is never about the person being abused, it is always about the abuser. **IT IS NOT PERSONAL TO YOU.**

It may help to find out more about the person who has done this to you. This may not be possible if it was done by a stranger or someone out of the family. If you can ask questions about the person's past, it will help you to see the bigger picture and how that person came to be and do what he or she did.

If the person who abused you was in the wider community, you could ask questions within that society. You may find that you are only one of a number of people to suffer at his hands. This is made easier by the Internet and e-mails. Sometimes it is easier to get a perspective on something if you are able to view it objectively rather than subjectively. You can do this by seeing someone who has gone through similar experiences and knowing that they are blameless and that their innocence is intact. This then must also apply to you!

FIND THE GIFTS

I believe that every experience we have in life, no matter how difficult or traumatic, provides us with great opportunities and gifts. Many people get so stuck in the negativity that they fail to see and utilise them.

The first opportunity will always be growth. We grow the most through the challenges that present us with big choices and life lessons. When life is uneventful, we do not look for answers. The first things we need to ask ourselves after any new experiences are:-

1) Did I enjoy this and would I want to repeat it? If the answer is no then we know we need to consciously decide not to. We may need to employ safeguards or tools to prevent a repeat of it.

2) If I did not like it then would I want to inflict this experience on anyone let alone someone that I love? Once again if the answer is no then a conscious

decision needs to be made not to project it onto anyone else.

3) I remove this experience from my unconscious mind and memory banks carrying forward only the lessons learned.

I also believe that the experiences we have in childhood can be the training ground we need for the life work we have come to do. For some people it may be directly related. For instance, a child who had a mentally ill parent may choose to work in mental health in some capacity. Who better to understand the issues involved. Other people may use the experiences of childhood to be a better parent than their parents were. By learning what did not work they look for a way that does.

The gifts provided by experiencing abuse first hand could go a long way to healing the world and removing these destructive patterns once and for all. To do this you have to be out of the victim mode. Some of the most powerful crusades were led by people who had suffered great adversity. I am not suggesting that everyone becomes a budding Joan of Arc but each person can do things to remove the legacy of abuse in the world.

Some suggestions are:-

1) Pass a new and positive legacy onto your children.

2) Raise awareness in the community.

3) Start an OSCA (Overcoming Sexual and Childhood Abuse.) support group. Get a couple or more people who have been through similar experiences together to work through the issues.

4) Do voluntary work with an organisation such as Childline to help children who are abused.

5) Make it your career to help or work with people who have been abused.

6) Write articles or your life story to inspire others and help them to overcome their abuse.

7) Lobby politicians to bring in safeguards to protect children.

8) Put your past behind you and CHOOSE to be happy.

SEE THE PERPETRATOR AS THE VICTIM

Part of the healing process of abuse is to change the perceptions that you took on at the time. When you are abused as a child you see the person doing this to you as being all powerful and you are helpless. As an adult you can begin to be aware of the patterns of abuse and what has gone on in the past that has brought the person to abuse.

This applies to all forms of abuse. The patterns that pass down remain fairly true. If a child did not receive love it may not be able to give or show it as a parent. If a person was beaten by his father or mother, he may believe that this is how to parent and do the same to his children.

In healing the abuse issue it may be necessary to see the person who perpetrated the abuse receiving the exact same treatment from its abuser and instead of feeling good about this, allow yourself to feel compassion and sorrow for the child experiencing this. You of all people know how it felt.

VISUALISATION

Take some time for yourself. Sit comfortably and take some deep breaths to relax the body and still the mind..... For each person who has abused you see them at the age you were when you were abused receiving the same treatment..... Allow yourself to empathise with their pain and struggle..... See yourself as you are now going to comfort that child..... You can feel genuine compassion, pity and even love for them..... See their innocence or vulnerability shining out..... You may want to empower them to say NO to what is being inflicted upon them..... Give them a hug but stipulate that you will not tolerate this behaviour from them..... Leave the situation feeling as if you are in command but at peace with that person and then bring your focus back into the room.

If this process brings up any negative feelings in you be sure to let them go by breathing them through and be aware that more work needs to be done on emotional release.

RESETTING THE BOUNDARIES

All forms of abuse break down our natural boundaries and allows a free for all. This is all on an unseen, unspoken level. We are all unconsciously responding to people's boundaries on a daily basis. We pick up the signals that the person is giving out and react accordingly.

There are two ways in which abuse affects our boundaries. It either annihilates them completely or we set such strong boundaries that no one can get near to us. Either way this is going to be detrimental to us in the end.

In this process you want to find the balance and reset the boundaries in a place that keeps you safe but open to allowing good things into your life and space.

1) Look at your patterns with boundaries. Are they very lax? This means that you allow people to treat you badly or do things that you do not want. Are they too strong? This will result in people giving you a wide berth and not approaching you. Do your boundaries fluctuate? Here you go from one extreme to another and people never know where they are with you.

2) Be aware that you have different types of boundaries. They can be physical, sexual or emotional. All of these need to be firmly set where you feel safe but do not deprive yourself of needed contact and support.

Take some time and space to reset your boundaries. Sit comfortably and take some deep breaths to relax the body and still the mind..... Command the unconscious mind to remove any boundaries that have been set in the past..... You are now going to be establishing new ones that can be programmed into the unconscious mind and memory banks..... See yourself on an empty beach with a wide expanse of smooth sand..... You have a stick in your hand..... The first boundary you are going to reset is the physical one..... Draw a circle in the sand where you feel that you are comfortable for people to be physically. This is your personal space and only those that you invite into that space may enter..... Press a set button in your mind..... Next is the sexual boundary..... You can allow your chosen sexual partners into this space but it must be at your instigation..... Draw the circle round you, making sure there are no gaps in it..... Press the set button..... Let your unconscious mind know that you are totally safe within these circles..... If anyone steps over the line you have only to say **NO** and they will retreat. Thank the unconscious for bringing in the new programming. When you are ready bring your attention back into the room.

BRINGING IN ACCEPTANCE

Acceptance is an essential stage in the healing process of abuse and many people are unable to move on without employing it. The first thing required in an Alcoholics Anonymous meeting is to accept that you have a problem. As soon as you are able to accept who you are and what happened, you can become who you want to be and create what you want to happen. If you do not, you get stuck in a fantasy that prevents you from living a real and normal life.

1) Are there aspects of your past that you are in denial over?

2) Do you dismiss what has happened or pretend that it has no significance for you?

3) Do you protect or excuse the person or people who abused you?

4) Are you able to accept yourself just as you are now?

5) Are you able to accept your abuser just as he/she is?

6) Can you accept that the people who should have protected you failed to do so?

7) Can you accept your anger, pain, guilt, fear and shame?

8) Can you accept the full impact of what the abuse has done in your life?

9) Can you accept all the positive things that have come out of your abuse?

If any of these areas create denial rather than acceptance then more work needs to be done to bring in acceptance. Create acceptance statements. Remember, what you resist persists. It can be things like:

I accept that I have been abused and that I have been playing a victim role.

Work up to I LOVE AND ACCEPT MYSELF JUST AS I AM.

Acceptance provides the spring board to move you forward and away from the destructive legacies of the past.

FINDING THE AUTHENTIC SELF

The authentic self is within us buried under a huge heap of damage and illusion that the facade is then designed to hide and mask.

1) What facades or roles have you adopted to show the world?

2) How would you like people to think you are?

3) What do you use this to cover over?

4) What would you least like people to know about you?

5) Do you have any sense of shame for these parts of you?

6) Do you keep you facade up all the time or are there some people that you show your damage to?

7) If you do let some people see it, how does it feel?

8) Are you aware of your authentic self?

9) What do you think it is like?

10) What would you like it to be like?

11) Can you imagine that if you were to remove your damage and dismantle your facade what it would be like to live your authentic life?

Finding and integrating your authentic self into your every day existence is a life long enterprise. It can only emerge when you no longer identify yourself with your damage and facade. I think that there is a protective mechanism that stores our damage in self-contained layers. As each layer surfaces you are able to process the emotions, beliefs and patterns and release them. This then makes way for the next layer to emerge and so on. You only get overwhelmed when a backlog is created by not processing the layers when they are presented. When enough damage has been removed, it will be safe to dismantle the fake facade and allow the authentic self to shine through.

The following visualisation is about resurecting the authentic self and can start the ball rolling in this long term project.

Take some time and space for yourself. Sit comfortably and take some deep breaths to relax the body and still the mind..... You are going to call in a symbolic representation of your facade, you will see it like the facade of a building on a film set..... The outside looks very real but it is made of plaster board and propped up by poles on the inside..... Note what your particular facade is like..... Is it big and flamboyant, ornate, simple, apologetic or shabby?..... See what characteristics it displays that you are wanting to show to the world..... Behind the facade is a space that is filled with the experiences and damage from childhood. This will be like a huge rubbish tip containing old junk and bin bags of putrid substances..... Note how high this tip is behind the facade..... Commit yourself to clearing out this rubbish heap and put the power of intention into doing so..... Call in a team of contractors to set the process in motion..... See them arrive with their hard hats and equipment..... See the skips ready to receive all the unwanted junk and cart it away.....

Supervise as these men begin to work from the top throwing all the rubbish away..... They may come across some treasures buried in the mess, these can be put aside and cleaned up..... As each skip fills up, it is removed and an empty one replaces is..... Do not feel tempted to hold onto or investigate any of the garbage, just let it go..... Gradually you will see the mass of stuff reduced to a manageable level..... You notice a door being revealed behind where the junk was..... Note what it looks like, how big it is and what it is made of..... When the last bits of rubbish have been removed and the contractors are gone it is time to resurect your authentic self..... See yourself going to the door and opening it..... Inside it is like an Egyptian tomb..... Your authentic self is lying on a stone slab in the centre in a state of suspended animation..... Take a powerful light source in with you and shine it onto the person..... See the light awaken your true self..... Turn the light up as high as it will go and see this amazing light filled being emerge..... Lead it out of the tomb and into full sunlight and see all parts of this being activate..... Get the contractors to demolish the facade...... See yourself merging with your authentic self..... Know that your authentic self is full of joy, fun, love, wisdom, creativity, beauty, peace, harmony and any number of other positive qualities..... Allow these to permeate into every area of your life..... When you are ready, bring your attention back into the room.

BRINGING IN FORGIVENESS

Forgiveness is the final hurdle in dealing with abuse issues. It can only occur when you are ready to leave the past behind and move on unencumbered by the baggage created within childhood.

Before forgiveness can take place the emotions of anger and guilt need to be processed and released.

1) Do you have any resistance to forgiving your abusers?

2) Do you feel as if your forgiveness is letting them off the hook for what they have done?

3) Can you see that forgiveness is a gift you are giving yourself in that it allows you to be free?

4) Make a list of the people you need to forgive, not forgetting the people who did not protect you and yourself.

5) With each one ask yourself if you are ready to let them go and forgive. If the answer is no, there is still some clearing to be done.

6) Start by writing a forgiveness letter to each person on the list. You do not need to send these off. Burn them once they are written. In certain situations you may choose to send it. Do not have any expectations as to what will happen. You may get a negative response back.

7) Know that forgiveness is not the words but the intention and state of being behind them. Check out whether you are feeling forgiving.

8) You may need to do the forgiving process a few times before you finally let go. You will know when this has occurred because there will be a sense of inner peace.

Take some time and space for yourself. Sit comfortably and take some deep breaths to relax the body and still the mind..... You are going to call in each person on your forgiveness list separately..... See each one a few feet in front of you facing you.... Say three times I FORGIVE YOU and if applicable I RELEASE YOU FROM MY LIFE..... Give them a gift that is beautifully wrapped. This contains your forgiveness..... See if there are any cords tying you to this person or the abuse..... Cut yourself free of them and as you do so see the person fading away..... They do not need to feature in your life unless you want them to..... Repeat this process with each person you need to forgive..... You are now going to give yourself the gift of forgiveness..... See the present with the bright paper and ribbons on it..... Unwrap it and find a beautiful white dove inside..... Take it in your cupped hands and launch it up into the sky..... Watch it fly free and unrestricted. This dove symbolises the peace and freedom that you so richly deserve..... See yourself looking out into your future..... There is nothing tying you to your past..... You carry forward only the lessons and gifts picked up on the way..... In your future lies all the wonderful things that you want to create..... Love, abundance, happiness, fulfilment, creativity and beauty..... This is yours just for being you..... When you are ready bring your attention back into the room and allow a sense of peace to take hold within.

FINAL NOTE

I believe that any issue that we have to face in life can be overcome and abuse certainly comes into this. However, if we do nothing then nothing will change. It does take desire and dedication to work on ourselves and make a difference. There are many forms of treatment and therapy that can help in this process but for those who are not willing to open up with someone I hope that some of the exercises and visualisations will help to let go of the past.

A support group can also make a big difference in working through abuse issues. It is very helpful to work with people who have been through similar experiences and seeing your situation from an objective view. If there is no such group in your area, you may want to set one up.

You may want to read this book again or repeat the exercises. You will find that you may get a completely different perspective on things once you have done some work on the issue.

Liz Adamson is available for talks, workshops and intensive 3 hour one to one sessions.

Contact: Flat 3, Hamptons, Hadlow, Tonbridge, Kent, TN11 9SR. Tel 07940 101918. Email liz@edenbook.co.uk

Also available by Liz Adamson

The 12 Principles of Optimal Living	£7.95
Relationships, A Journey into Wholeness	£7.95
Abundance and Prosperity.	£7.95
The Ultimate Guides to Emotional Freedom	
Releasing Anger	£4.95
Releasing Hurt and Sadness	£4.95
Embracing Love	£4.95
Embracing Happiness	£4.95

The Secrets of Optimal Living inspiration cards £7.95

All above titles soon available on high quality CDs

Available from Diviniti Publishing. Tel 01732 220373
Website: www.hypnosisaudio.com

Also available from Diviniti Publishing best selling hypnosis tapes and CDs including:

Complete Relaxation

Lose Weight Now

Heal Your Body and many others.